Grades **K-1**

Linda Hoyt and
Teresa Therriault

# Mastering *the* Mechanics

Ready-to-Use Lessons for Modeled, Guided, and Independent Editing

**SCHOLASTIC**

NEW YORK • TORONTO • LONDON • AUCKLAND • SYDNEY
MEXICO CITY • NEW DELHI • HONG KONG • BUENOS AIRES

Credits
Rebecca Sitton's High-Frequency Writing Words and High-Frequency Patterns/Rimes

Cover design by Jay Namerow
Interior design by Maria Lilja
Interior photos by Linda Hoyt, Teresa Therriault, and Patrick Burke
Acquiring editor: Lois Bridges
Production editor: Erin K. L. Grelak
Copy Editor: David Klein
ISBN 13: 978-0-545-04877-4
ISBN 10: 0-545-04877-X

We dedicate this to our husbands, Steve and Darrel. They make us smile, support us in countless ways, and love to remind us how lucky we are to have their love and support. They are right. We are wonderfully lucky to have them. Thanks, guys!

# ACKNOWLEDGMENTS

We feel fortunate to have worked together for many years as Title I teachers, staff developers, and friends. Through these years, we have had many mentors along the way who have helped us lift our practice, challenge our thinking, and find the courage to reach beyond what we knew yesterday. Those mentors include our colleagues, the children we have had the honor to serve, and those powerful professionals whose books on writing constantly challenge and inform us. Donald Graves, Donald Murray, Shelley Harwayne, Lucy Calkins, Regie Routman, Ralph Fletcher, Katie Wood Ray, and many others have carried the torch and helped us all make a bigger difference for young writers.

At Kinnaman Elementary in Beaverton, Oregon, Jan McCall, principal, opened her heart and the classrooms of her wonderful learning community so that we could capture the photos that appear in this resource and on the cover. Their beautiful children, led by Marie Davis, Melissa Suesserman, Angie Thomas, Heidi Cochran, Traci Orth, and Patty Jo Foley, stretched our thinking and confirmed the validity of these cycles.

The lessons in this resource were carefully tested to ensure they were classroom-ready and reflective of the challenges young editors face. Piloting educators included district administrators, teachers, principals, and consultants. Their feedback to the learning cycles put muscle behind our thinking through their insightful observations of learners and helpful suggestions. In Davidson County, North Carolina, our heartfelt thanks go to Sonja Parks, April Willard, Wendy Younts, Leigh Ann Bruff, Amber Idol, Amber Parker, Stephanie Ward, Tricia Prevette, and Emily Lipe. In Ukiah, California, we thank Kathryn McInnis, Debbee Freeman, Cathy Hessom, Gayle Kline, Janet McLeod, Caryl Mastrof, and Leslie Maricle-Barclay for opening their thinking and their classrooms to engage with the lessons. Kelly Boswell and Barbara Coleman, master teachers and independent consultants, provided valuable affirmations and encouragement.

We have found it quite joyous to get to know the team at Scholastic. Lois Bridges, our amazing editor and trusted friend, is a cherished anchor, always smoothing the way with careful suggestions, time-saving support, and unflagging optimism. Eagle-eye "Grammar Goddess" Gloria Pipkin is our indispensable safety net. Terry Cooper, Ray Coutu, David Klein, Maria Lilja, and Erin K. L. Grelak have generously shared their thinking, expanded our vision, and helped this resource take shape in the teacher-friendly manner we so wished to achieve. It has been a pleasure, and we thank them sincerely.

# TABLE OF CONTENTS

To print out the reproducibles at full size in the Tools, Assessment and Record Keeping, and Appendix: Student Writing Samples sections, please visit www.scholastic.com/masteringthemechanics.

# PART I

# Introduction: Mastering the Mechanics

## Putting Editing in Perspective

**W**e care about the conventions of written language, and we are not alone. The parents of the children we serve, the community, and the public all care about and expect children to show growing expertise in the conventions of written language and to present written work in such a way that it is legible; spelled correctly; and demonstrates correct grammar, capitalization, and punctuation.

As we focus young learners on mechanics and conventions, we want to be very clear about our goals:

1. To nurture writers who understand that rich, well-crafted messages are our first and most important focus.

2. To help children understand that a study of mechanics and conventions is about *adding tools* that enhance our messages, not just about correcting and being "right."

It is important to state that we are not in favor of prepackaged programs that cast editing and conventions as "mistakes" or exercises in correction. These programs have very little embedded instruction and consistently overwhelm students with sentences that are so laden with errors that meaning is easily lost, leaving a writer with few connections to his or her own work.

> **"**Just as the baker who creates a cake from scratch takes pride in adding butter-cream roses atop chocolate swirls, students must learn to delight in knowing how to add the important touches of correct spelling, grammar, and punctuation.**"**
> —*Shelley Harwayne*

**conventions**
(spacing, handwriting, spelling, and grammar)

**mechanics**
(periods, capital letters, and so on)

Above all, as we cast our attention upon mechanics and conventions, we must be sure that creative thinking flourishes during drafting and revision. If mechanics and editing are overemphasized, they can have the negative effect of reducing writing volume, causing children to limit their writing to words they are able to spell correctly or to use overly simplistic sentence structures.

# Recast Mechanics and Conventions as Tools to Lift Writing Quality

Writers must understand that mechanics are not tedious obligations. They are tools that add clarity and interest to our writing. Carefully crafted modeled writing lessons improve craft, mechanics, grammar, and spelling. Our goal is to develop the understanding that writers integrate mechanics into craft rather than seeing them simply as elements of "correctness." A modeled writing with a think-aloud recasting mechanics as craft might sound like this:

> I want to write about how quiet it was when I was walking in the woods. I could say: "I went walking in the woods. It was quiet." That is okay, but if I think about how punctuation can help me write in more interesting ways, I think I can make it even better.
>
> What do you think of: "Shhh! Listen! As my feet crunch softly on the gravel path, the sound seems huge. It is so quiet in the forest that my footsteps sound <u>loud</u>!" Look how I used exclamation points. That helped my opening and my ending to be more interesting. And do you see the comma I used? That told my reader to take a little breath so the ending of my sentence is more dramatic. Using punctuation makes my writing better!

It is our sincere hope that this resource will help educators and children alike see conventions and mechanics through new eyes. We believe conventions and mechanics are naturally woven into the writing process at two major points:

1. During drafting: Conventions and mechanics support our messages and enhance communication. Carefully chosen punctuation can clarify, control volume and flow, plus make ideas sparkle!

2. During editing: Conventions and mechanics provide readers with access to our thinking. Correct spelling, grammar, spacing, and punctuation make our work accessible to readers.

## Highlight Mechanics and Conventions in Mentor Texts

We have become accustomed to turning to wonderful mentor texts to enrich children's exposure to literary language, form, and craft. Children's literature is also one of our most powerful tools for celebrating and noting the interesting ways in which writers use spacing, punctuation, capitalization, and grammar. Encouraging children to reread and look closely at a familiar text helps them attend to the fine points, noticing the frequency of end-punctuation marks, spacing, or purposes for capital letters. Using literature to present mechanics provides a tapestry of opportunity in which to explore mechanics, while helping children to understand that *all writers* think about spacing, grammar, punctuation, spelling, and so on.

Compare the use of question marks across favorite selections.

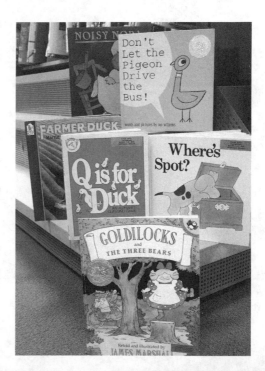

Reread to notice spaces between words.

Clear acetate overlays allow children to trace conventions right in a book.

Rereading familiar favorites to count question marks and periods heightens awareness of conventions in print.

Shared reading is a perfect time to highlight the ways in which authors use conventions.

# Focus on Reading and Writing as Reciprocal Processes

Reading and writing are reciprocal language processes (Clay, 2005; Gentry, 2007). As writers create text, they are constantly rereading their work and applying all they know about how print works. When writers read, they take in models of language, spacing, conventional spelling, and punctuation that will inform their own work as writers. Reading and writing are powerful partners, extending and transforming the network of literacy understandings our youngest learners are constructing. The key is to make this reciprocal relationship transparent to our students.

**❚❚Participation in strong writing programs clearly benefits both reading and writing development.❚❚**
—*Donald Graves*

# Modeling: The Heart of Our Work

We believe it is critical to do a great deal of modeled writing as the children observe and listen to us think out loud about conventions and mechanics and how they are woven into our messages. We *show* writers how we use letters, sounds, punctuation, and grammar to make our thinking accessible to a reader. We believe that, every day, children should have the chance to observe the creation of quality writing that has artistic punctuation, jaw-dropping phrasing, and sets a model that they can attempt to emulate.

Explicit demonstrations of writing are central to the work we do as writing coaches. When we model interesting openings, insertion of onomatopoeia with an exclamation point, or how to write items in a list, we are clarifying our students' vision of quality writing.

## Think Out Loud During Modeled Writing

The think-alouds we provide during modeled writing make the inner workings of the writing process transparent to children. If we allow our thoughts to flow around the creation of text, children can listen in as we make decisions about word choice, spelling, punctuation, and grammar. Let children ride with you on your writing journey as you construct and deconstruct your thinking. There is nothing more powerful than watching you, their teacher, think out loud about words and letters, and then pause midstream to reread and see how everything is coming together; or model how to go back and add letters, insert words, or give the spelling of a particular word a second try.

**Never ask students to do something they haven't watched you do first.**

Think-alouds during modeled writing open the door to the wonders that occur as we think, write, reread, and then write again. Think-alouds show learners how we massage a message to make our ideas come alive on paper.

## Model Rereading and Marking Up a Text

Help students understand that after our message is complete and we begin to edit, our work may look a bit messy. We may cross out words and try a different spelling, change a lowercase letter to a capital letter, and so on. This is okay! This is what editors do, and a text marked up well means the "editor" is doing a good job!

## Model Using "Band-Aids"

We generally do not ask kindergarten and first-grade children to recopy their work to create a final draft. Instead, we provide strips of correction tape when over-erasing or multiple cross-outs have created an unreadable smudge. Rolls of correction tape come in many widths and are easily available at office supply stores. Many first-grade and kindergarten writers, enjoy putting these "Band-Aids" on their work when erasures have become a challenge during editing. Young children take great delight in watching the teacher model putting "Band-Aids" on a piece of modeled writing during revision and editing.

# Joys of Early Writing

Writing time with kindergartners and first graders is a joyous time, filled with wonder, discovery, and learning. We all celebrate the magic of writing that first appears as drawing, then labeling. . . then the first bursts of connected words on a page. With each day, "writing" and the "writer" take on new dimensions, gaining strength, fluency, and confidence. How exciting it is to survey writing samples and see the visible evidence of growth in phonics, sentence structure, meaning, and mechanics!

The conventional writing shown on these samples is placed on a sticky note. Teachers do not write directly on the children's papers.

## The Importance of Approximation

During children's first tentative interactions with paper and pen, we encourage experimentation and approximation. Writing strategies such as "write the first letter and draw a line for the rest of the word" or "write the sounds you know" free children to focus on ideas and support the development of both meaning and spelling. These strategies for independence free writers to "keep writing," rather than becoming stuck on the spelling of an unknown word. This is critical if we

are to create resourceful and independent writers who realize that waiting in line for the teacher to provide the spelling of an unknown word will cause them to lose track of their thought and create an unnecessary dependency that wastes learning time. But again, we must model.

## Modeling Word Construction

While modeling word construction, we slowly and deliberately stretch out words, saying them slowly so we can hear the sounds. We model how to write the beginning sound and draw a line for the rest of the word when we aren't sure of the rest.

> Boys and girls, I had the most wonderful banana split on my birthday! I want to write *banana*, so I will say the word really slowly. It starts with /b/. I am going to use my picture alphabet card to help myself and write the letter *b*. I am not sure of the rest of the word, so I am going to draw a line for now and think about the rest later so I don't forget my idea.

We continue writing and thinking aloud, joyfully returning to *banana* when we think of more letters we can incorporate to make the word closer to the conventional spelling.

> Oh! I remembered more sounds I can use in *banana*! I want to add /n/ and /a/. Those are at the end of banana. I am going to go back to that word and add *n* and *a*. That's better!

**L**ucy Calkins and Natalie Louis (2003) remind us that it is crucial to let children in on a secret, that "sometimes we can't read their stories because of spelling and handwriting."

# Thinking About Audience

Children need to learn that one of the reasons we write is to share our writing with others. With an audience in mind, authors must think about the message *plus* conventions (spacing, handwriting, spelling, and grammar) and mechanics (periods, capital letters, and so on). When there is an authentic audience, authors have strong and viable purposes for looking more closely at their work and expecting more from the print they create.

To build a sense of audience, we believe it is important to provide authentic reasons for students to share their writing. Activities such as partner sharing, author's chair, end-of-workshop sharing circles, and publishing all help. But we can go further. If we make students' writing public as often as possible, a sense of audience elevates in importance. With this in mind, we invite kindergarten and first-grade students to do the following:

- Write notes to each other and the teacher.
- Write letters to the principal, the cook, or the school secretary.
- Write letters to their parents and ask them to write back.
- Create partnerships with another class so they can read their writing to a different authentic audience.
- Publish their work as class books and individual books.
- Post writing on the walls of the classroom.
- Make signs to label walls, doors, and paper towel dispensers, or to remind us of processes and procedures.
- Write notes for authentic purposes, using "From the Desk of _____" pads.

> **"** Students can hear all we have to say about punctuation, but if there are no real-life connections, little will stick. **"**
> —*Janet Angelillo*

Keegan writes a note to the teacher, "I like my air hockey table." Andy wrote a note to his mother after he remembered he used the last of the toothpaste while getting ready for school. "From the Desk of _____" examples are in the tools section on page 162.

Authentic audience and authentic purposes work hand in hand to provide the motivation and a rationale for why conventions and mechanics are important. This is the time when we reread for "correctness" and for lifting the visual aspects of our message to the highest possible levels.

# The Classroom Environment

The environment we create for writing is important. A rich environment for writing should have areas for:

**Modeled writing and sharing**

**Editing conferences and coaching for individuals**

**Shared thinking and partner editing**

The walls should make strong statements about the learning in the classroom. Modeled writing, word walls, editing checklists, and posters showing studies of conventions should be clearly visible.

With a grin of sheer delight, I lifed the warm, gooey cookie to my lips. Mmmm Good!

Pop! Sizzle! Zing! The heated kernels vibrated madly as they prepared to explode. Boom! Like a bomb, it goes kaboom.

**Modeled writing should be available for children to revisit over time. It can become a source of familiar words and strategies as well as a resource to model continued editing and expansion of language.**

**Word walls and lists of frequently used words should be positioned so that children can reach the words and touch individual letters.**

Interactive posters, built collaboratively with children, make strong statements about the importance of conventions and mechanics in published literature and in our own work as writers.

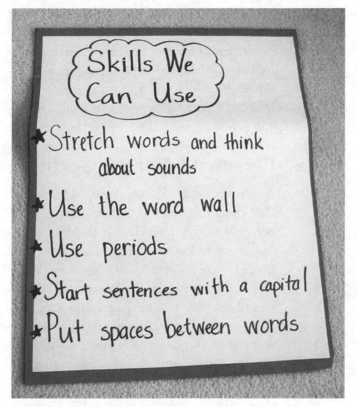

**Editing checklists should emphasize children's current phase of development and change over time to reflect new learning.**

## Model the Use of Classroom Tools

When classroom walls reflect a rich tapestry of writing forms, tools, and supports, a strong message is sent to children, parents, and our colleagues that this is a classroom where writing and mechanics are celebrated and savored. It is important to remember, however, that rich visuals provide invitations, but real use will occur only with explicit and careful modeling of the tools in action.

**Visuals are only helpful if students actively use them.**

We believe that we must model the use of word walls, charts, and environmental print so children understand that we minimize the use of these tools during drafting and emphasize their use when we edit for an audience. We must also demonstrate that the role of our personal tools is different. We use personal tools continuously during all phases of writing.

## Picture Alphabet Cards and Personal Alphabet Strips

Writers need personal tools such as a well-organized writing folder in which they store their work, and their personal alphabet strips or picture alphabet cards as support for constructing words. These tools need to be right in front of writers as they draft. Alphabet strips at the 10-foot level are of little use to a kindergarten or first-grade writer. Personal alphabet strips and personal picture alphabet cards are as essential as pencils and paper.

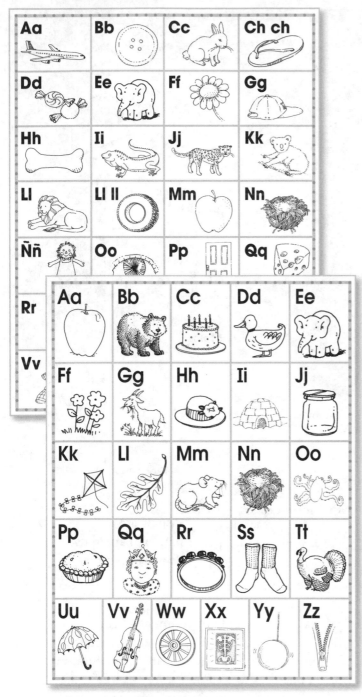

As you plan your modeled writing sessions, please do integrate the use of picture alphabet cards or sentence strips into your writing demonstrations and think-alouds. If children see you using the tool effectively, they will soon be moving toward independence with these important tools.

## Personal Editing Checklists

As writers begin shifting from an editing checklist in a poster format to using personal editing checklists, it will be important to ensure that the checklist matches writer levels of development. You will find examples in the assessment and record-keeping section, pages 165 and 166. While these examples may offer needed matches to the levels of some of your students, please consider creating your own editing checklists that match up with the skills students are learning and the cycles you have selected for instruction.

**Strategies Good Editors Use**
- [ ] Reread for every editing point
- [ ] Check capital letters
- [ ] Notice punctuation:
    - [ ] Periods
    - [ ] Exclamation points
    - [ ] Question marks
    - [ ] Commas
    - [ ] Apostrophe
- [ ] Use resources to check my spelling

_____

(author)          (editing partner)          (date)

**English and Spanish personal picture alphabet cards are resources that empower writers. See Tools, pages 158 and 159.**

**The picture alphabet cards are designed to provide instruction for the letters of the alphabet and the sounds most commonly associated with those letters, including sounds represented by individual consonants and the long and short sounds represented by vowels; however, there are many other sounds that letters can represent, which might become the focus of a word study you conduct with your students.**

# Writing Folders and Skills I Can Use Lists

In designing folders, we believe it is very helpful to include a sheet of paper titled "Skills I Can Use" attached to one side of the folder. This sheet becomes a record of the skills each individual learner can control as a writer. Each time we have an editing conference and work on a convention, or a mechanic or a spelling strategy, we add the skill to the Skills I Can Use list. This list is an ongoing personal reminder to the learner and the teacher that the skill has been mastered. Children learn that once a skill has been added to their list, we expect them to apply that skill in every piece of writing written for an audience.

**When writers have a well-organized writing folder, writing and personal tools are easily accessible.**

| Skills I Can Use | |
|---|---|
| Skills used in my writing | I started using this on date_____ |
| | |
| | |
| | |
| | |
| | |
| | |
| | |
| | |
| | |

PART V: ASSESSMENT AND RECORD KEEPING • 169

**Writing folders should have a place where learners can record skills or conventions they can use as writers. Once items are on their personal list, writers know that they are accountable to work on these skills every time they edit. See page 168 for a template.**

# When Do We Start Focusing on Mechanics and Conventions?

A common question is, "When does a focus on mechanics and conventions begin?" We prefer a question such as "How do mechanics and conventions *evolve* with our youngest writers?" If we see a sense of audience and mechanics as something that develops over time, it is easier to see how we might keep the focus on meaning while steeping learners in modeled writing and gently guiding them toward conventions and audience. With this emphasis, it would be perfectly natural to have a modeled writing lesson that sounds something like:

> I love popcorn. I love the crackly crunch and poppety pop as kernels start to explode. One of the things I love is that the "pop" sometimes surprises me. I am going to use exclamation points to show that in my writing. Watch to see how I use exclamation points to make my writing more interesting. My first word is *pop* (p-o-p). First, I write the letters, and then I add the exclamation point (!).

> "Pop! Pop! Poppety! I can hardly wait for those salty, crunchy bits to land on my tongue."

By recasting punctuation as a tool that can make our writing sparkle, we have maintained a clear focus on meaning. This kind of work on mechanics and conventions is developmentally appropriate *right from the start.*

## Tiptoe Lightly With "Correctness"

We must avoid a situation in which a fear of being incorrect freezes writers and forces them into a narrow zone of "correctness." In this kind of setting, children can sometimes place too much emphasis on spelling, for example, and begin to limit their writing to words they know they can spell correctly. This is dangerous, as then the writing is guided by spelling rather than the writer's sense of language and imagination. While empowering writers with conventions, we must also take seriously our mission to keep meaning as the primary objective. Our goal: for language to be lifted and elaborated, with mechanics as a subset of the message.

**Conventions and mechanics should support meaning, not limit it.**

We do believe, however, that it is appropriate to set expectations and to make it clear to children that after completing a cycle, they have new tools that they can use and that they are expected to use. After a lesson on putting your name on your paper, it is perfectly reasonable to expect writers to do so. After a lesson on rereading to add more letters, it is reasonable to expect writers to reread and think about the letters they have used. As we tiptoe, we can still have high expectations for our students' development and growth.

**❚❚ The last thing you want is for your children to settle for 'The dog bit at me,' instead of writing "the dog snarled at me," because of a concern for correctness. ❚❚**

*—Lucy Calkins and Natalie Louis*

# Rereading: Strategic Tool for Meaning, Mechanics, and Conventions

- Rereading during *drafting* helps our ideas flow and helps us regain momentum with the message we are crafting.

- Rereading during *revision* helps us wonder about craft elements such as word choice, interesting leads, voice, volume, and focus of information. It is also a time when we can wonder if our punctuation is used in ways that help the reader, add clarity to our thinking, or make the writing more interesting.

- Rereading when we *edit for an audience* takes on an entirely different dimension. This is the time when we slow down and really look at the visual characteristics of what we have created.

## Rereading: Focused Edits

When young children reread to edit and check for conventions and mechanics, we believe it is most effective if you have them engage in focused edits. In a focused edit, the writer reads with a focus on a single purpose. For example, the writer might reread once to check for end punctuation. Then, the writer rereads again to check for capital letters. Each editing point gets its own rereading. Focused edits with a single purpose for each rereading help writers keep a clear focus on their purpose. This keeps them from becoming distracted or overwhelmed by simultaneous purposes.

## Rereading Power

- What do I see?
- Is the writing neat enough for someone else to read?
- Are there spaces between words so a reader can tell where words start and stop?
- Do my picture and my words make good use of space on the page?
- Does my punctuation add to the message?
- Did I use a capital letter to start my sentence?
- How is the spelling?
- What words should I revisit?

*"Rereading is the glue that connects the stages of writing. Writers continually reread what they've written, and this rereading changes at each stage of the craft cycle."*
—*Ralph Fletcher and JoAnn Portalupi*

**First focused edit: Reread for spacing. Reread again *through a new lens* to try to add more letters to words.**

You can bring an element of fun into the focused edits by providing an array of inexpensive "reading" glasses. Putting on the glasses and seeing the writing *through a new lens* helps young writers understand how closely we read when we are editing.

# The Teaching/Assessing Loop

Assessment is our essential guide to quality instruction. As we observe writers during drafting, meeting with them in small groups or conferring with individuals, we are constantly assessing to determine what they do and do not know. Our assessments are the best possible guides to instruction. The data we gather through thoughtful, sensitive assessment help us choose the next skills our students need and also help us determine whether our students are fully grasping the material we're teaching.

## Selecting Skills for Instruction

To determine which conventions and mechanics are expected at a particular grade level, look first at your state standards. We suggest that you consider highlighting these standards on a photocopy of the Skills Continuum located on page 30. If you are working with a mandated language arts resource, you might identify the skills for spelling, punctuation, grammar, and so on, in the program and then highlight those on the grid as well. (We like to add program-driven goals in a second color so we can see where they deviate from state standards.) Now, as you look at the grid, you have a unified picture that shows state standards and program requirements in a single, easy-to-follow format that will round out your editing work with kindergarten and first-grade students. Secondly, assess the skills your students are already implementing in their writing.

## Assess the Skills Your Students Can Use

We find it immensely helpful to collect *unedited* writing samples and use the Class Record-Keeping Grid provided in assessment, page 170. It takes only minutes to list students' names in the first column and jot down target conventions and mechanics across the top of the other columns. With a stack of writing samples in hand, you are ready to start placing check marks for writers who show evidence of adequate space between words, as well as periods, capitals, and so on. Make several copies of the grid with students' names recorded. As you expand your assessment of additional skills and strategies, your grid is ready.

Once you have a profile of your students and their needs, you are ready to select a cycle and begin "Mastering the Mechanics!"

In the "I Love My Mom" example on page 25, our assessment review shows that this writer uses spaces between words and stretches writing across the entire line. While there are some capital letters in place, we would want to see additional samples to be sure that capitalization is being used consciously. There are no periods in place, so on the grid, we check off "spaces between words" and "uses entire line." Then, we place a dot for "period at the end of a sentence," to indicate that this would be a helpful learning target for this writer.

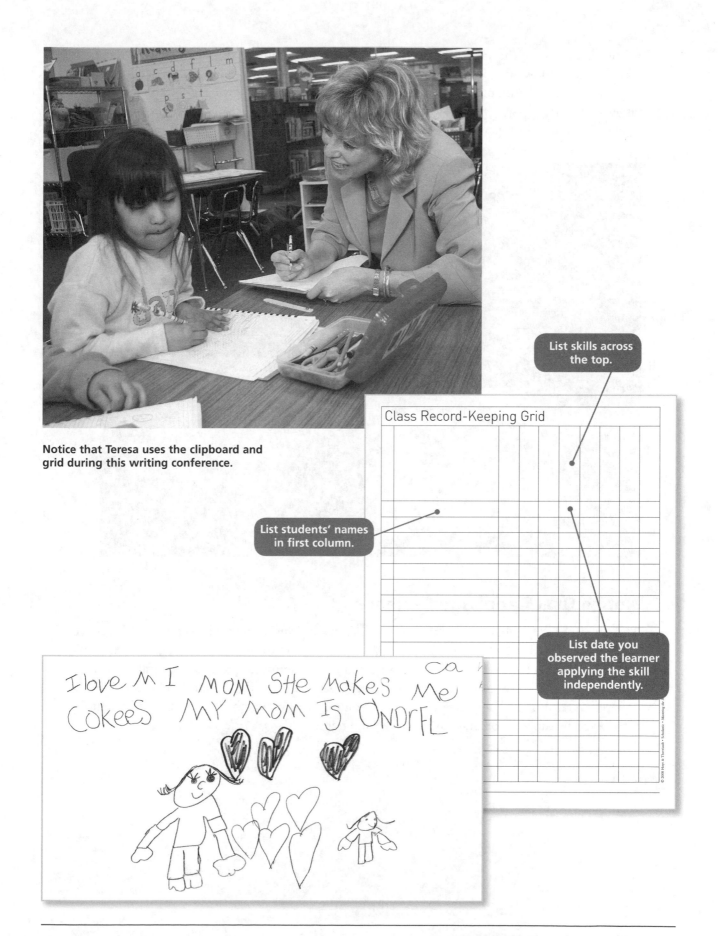

Notice that Teresa uses the clipboard and grid during this writing conference.

Class Record-Keeping Grid

**List skills across the top.**

**List students' names in first column.**

**List date you observed the learner applying the skill independently.**

I love M I mom she makes me cokees my mom is ONDrFL

With the use of the grid, a quick review of unedited writing exposes patterns of need. The grid also allows us to quickly identify groups of writers who share similar needs as editors. Because of this assessment, we can quickly and easily gather small groups for explicit instruction targeted directly to their needs. We find this assessment so helpful that we keep it on a clipboard while circulating during writer's workshop, and as a reference during writing conferences.

## Notice Oral Language Patterns

The grammar usage that appears in young children's writing is tightly linked to oral language. With this in mind, we challenge ourselves to *listen* carefully to notice which children are still struggling with subject-verb agreement, verb tenses, or the use of pronouns in oral speech. In addition to consciously listening to oral language patterns, we take dictation. This provides a concrete record of oral language patterns and quickly shows which children might benefit from some explicit support for oral language development.

# A Note About Editing Checklists

Editing checklists in kindergarten and first grade begin as a poster on the wall that may be as simple as this one:

> **Is your name on your paper?**
>
> **Use the date stamp.**
>
> **Reread your work.**
>
> **See if you can add more letters or words.**

As proficiency grows and students get used to editing as the last step in writing, you might want to transition to an editing checklist that writers actually fill out. You will find examples in the assessment section of this resource, pages 165 and 166.

**It is important to remember that editing checklists do not "teach"; they simply remind students to use the processes that you have modeled.**

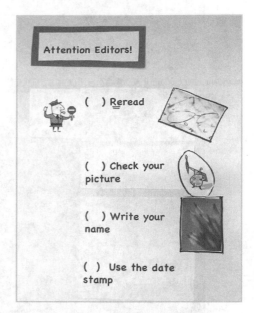

**Editing checklists grow and change in response to writer development.**

# Editing Conferences: Adding the Chocolate Swirls

We teach writers that if they are going to have an audience for their writing, they need to follow these last steps as editors:

Assuming that you have already held a revision conference with the writer, an editing conference provides a second opportunity for you and the writer to think together about a particular piece of writing. The first time, the emphasis is on craft, including the use of interesting punctuation to lift the writing. This time, the focus of the conference is editing.

During this conference, you will want to select one or two skills to address with the child. Never teach more than one or two things; children usually cannot retain that much information. We like to keep sticky notes on hand during editing conferences, in accordance with our belief that when writers make their own corrections and retain control of the pencil, they are more likely to remember and reuse what they have learned.

## Steps for Editors

If you have revised your work and are sure the message is just the way you want it, you are ready to:

1. Use the editing checklist. Do a focused edit for each item on the list.

2. Find an editing partner. Read the writing together and think about making it the best it can be.

3. Sign up for an editing conference with the teacher.

With this in mind, an editing conference might sound something like the following:

Anna, you must be so pleased that you have decided to publish your piece on giving your dog a bath. As a reader, I could totally visualize the soapy mess that you AND the dog made during this particular bath. What a great job you did in explaining the bubbles and the water.

As we begin editing, please tell me what you and your editing partner have already discovered and worked on in your writing. Be sure to point out any changes or additions you and your editing partner were able to make.

I see that you have underlined six words that you want to look at for spelling. Please show me the two you most want to work on today. Great! Let's look closely at *soapy* and *fur*. We can use your Portable Word Wall (see Tools, page 160) so you can save these words that are special to you. I will use these sticky notes to write the correct spelling for some other words and place them on your paper so you can finish editing the spelling after our conference.

### Remember Focused Edits

Simultaneous rereading for every element on a checklist can be too great of a challenge and result in less effective editing. Each item on an editing checklist should get its own focused edit. If there are four items on the checklist, writers will reread at least four times.

# The Yearlong Planner

The Yearlong Planner featured on the gatefold (the inside front cover) of this book is a tool to help you map out your curriculum for mechanics and conventions for the year. As you can see, this planner provides week-by-week suggestions for three content cycles, followed by a Pulling It All Together cycle to solidify the learning with authentic, interactive purpose. During a Pulling It All Together cycle, no new skills are added. This is a time for learners to apply their learning of the previous cycles in authentic contexts. With this plan as your guide, students will have four weeks of instruction and plentiful opportunities to transfer the skills learned to long-term memory.

Please note that a blank version of the Yearlong Planner is provided on page 171. With this planner, you can use your assessments of learners, along with your own state standards, to build a personalized curriculum map.

**Important Note:** This planner does not contain all of the lessons in this resource. We built a wide range of lessons to support your responses to the needs of your students. There are many paths through this resource. You may elect to use all of the planner or portions of it, or you can select lessons entirely based upon the needs of your learners. The choices and the path you take are up to you.

# On Your Way!

The instructional cycles that are the centerpiece of this resource are meant to celebrate writers and their ever-growing control over craft and form. As you enter these cycles, we challenge you to recast conventions and mechanics as tools for enhancing meaning and to have a joyous journey as you and your students begin "Mastering the Mechanics!"

# PART II

# Skills
# Continuum

The skills continuum profiles the spectrum of development in mechanics and conventions that might be expected from learners in the elementary grades. For ease of use, it is divided into sections that match the organizational structure of the lessons.

Each convention listed on the continuum is supported by an explanation that often includes an example for clarity. To the right of each listed convention is a designation of grade level(s) at which writers should be exposed to and learn to implement the convention. When a convention is supported by a lesson in this resource, the page number on which the lesson appears is also listed.

You may find it helpful to photocopy the continuum and keep a copy on a clipboard. This way the continuum can serve in the following ways:

## Sections

Processes Editors Use

Spacing

Capitalization

Punctuation

Spelling

Grammar

- a quick reference when planning your own mini-lessons or cycles of support for conventions

- a valuable reference when conferring with students during writing conferences

- a place to highlight and keep track of times when you provide mini-lessons on a convention

Overall, the continuum should offer a broad-based view of your students' writing development across a range of mechanics, conventions, and processes that good editors use, and empower your thinking as you differentiate instruction for the range of learners you serve.

| Page where lesson appears in this book | Conventions & Mechanics | Explanation | K | 1 | 2 | 3 | 4 | 5 |
|---|---|---|---|---|---|---|---|---|
| | | **PROCESSES EDITORS USE** | | | | | | |
| 40 | **Putting your name on the paper** | Writers should habitualize writing their names on papers before creating text or drawings. | • | • | | | | |
| 42 | **Counting the words in a message** | Before writing, young writers count the words in their message to match speech to print. | • | • | | | | |
| 44 | **Reread and touch each word** | Writers touch each word to check for omissions. | • | • | • | | | |
| | **Reread to focus on message** | Meaning is always our first emphasis when creating text. Writers must reread to confirm or revise for meaning before focusing on surface conventions. | • | • | • | • | • | • |
| | **Reread to edit for conventions** | Once meaning is clear, writers reread to check for surface structures and grammar that give our writing uniformity. | • | • | • | • | • | • |
| 46 | **Focused edit: reread for each editing point** | Rereading helps writers check for surface structures and grammar. The piece is read once for each editing point. | • | • | • | • | • | • |
| 48 | **Using an editing checklist** | Checklists matched to developmental levels of writers are used to guide personal and partner edits. | • | • | • | • | • | • |
| | **Use copyediting symbols to support editing** | Authors and editing partners use standardized copyediting symbols to identify and support their editorial work. | | | | • | • | • |
| | **Edit with a partner** | When partners work together to proofread, they elevate each other's thinking about text. | • | • | • | • | • | • |
| | **Celebrate and self-reflect** | To grow, writers must take time to reflect on their own growth as communicators of meaning. | • | • | • | • | • | • |
| | | **CONVENTIONS FOR SPACING** | | | | | | |
| 52 | **Word boundaries: keep letters in a word close together** | Letters in a word need to be clustered so word boundaries are apparent. | • | • | | | | |
| 54 | **Using entire page** | Writers should write from top to bottom, left to right, using return sweep. | • | • | | | | |

| Page | Topic | Description | | | | | | |
|---|---|---|---|---|---|---|---|---|
| 56 | **Using multiple pages** | Writers need to expand their thinking beyond single-page writing experiences. | • | • | • | • | • | • |
| | **Margins** | Allow appropriate margin, headers, and footer spaces. | • | • | • | • | • | • |
| | **Pagination in a multiple-page piece** | Page breaks are governed by arrangement around visuals and by available space on a page. Each page in a story should have a page number. | • | • | • | • | • | • |
| | **Spacing of visuals in nonfiction** | Visuals carry important messages in nonfiction and can appear in many positions on a page. | • | • | • | • | • | • |
| | **Placement of nonfiction features** | Nonfiction features such as the table of contents, captions, headings, index, and glossary have their own conventions for spacing. | • | • | • | • | • | • |
| | **Paragraph breaks** | Paragraphs should be arranged on a page so they are clearly set apart from one another. | | | • | • | • | • |
| | **Spacing in a letter** | Spacing for friendly and business letters follows a uniform format for the date, greeting, closing, and signature. | | • | • | • | • | • |
| | **Spacing on an envelope** | Envelopes have clearly defined spaces for the addressee and the return address. | | | • | • | • | • |

## CAPITALIZATION

| Page | Topic | Description | | | | | | |
|---|---|---|---|---|---|---|---|---|
| | **Capitalize the pronoun "I"** | I am going to Anna's house. | • | • | • | • | • | • |
| 114 | **Use mostly lowercase letters** | Capital letters need to be used for specific purposes. | • | • | | | | |
| 116 | **Capitalize the beginning of sentences** | Capitalize the first word in each sentence. | • | • | • | • | • | • |
| 118 | **Capitalize proper nouns: names and places** | My sister, Anna, is taking dance lessons in Seattle. She hopes to perform at the Keller Auditorium. | • | • | • | • | • | • |
| | **Capitalize a title before a name** | Mrs. Jones works in the office of Judge Jacobs | • | • | • | • | | |
| | **Capitalize proper adjectives** | Proper adjectives are formed from a noun used as an adjective: American figure skaters, French bread. | | | | • | • | • |
| 120 | **Capitalize days of the week** | Monday, Tuesday | • | • | • | • | • | |
| 122 | **Capitalize titles** | *Where the Wild Things Are, My Swimming Party* | • | • | • | • | • | • |

| # | Skill | Example | | | | | | |
|---|---|---|---|---|---|---|---|---|
| | **Capitalize for emphasis** | HOORAY! | | • | • | • | • | • |
| | **Capitalize AM and PM** | Abbreviations for morning and afternoon need to be capitalized when they are written without a period. | | | • | • | • | • |
| | **Capitalize abbreviations for state names (OR, CA, NY)** | Names of states are abbreviated with two capital letters. | | | • | • | • | • |
| | **Common nouns can become proper nouns** | A common noun, used as a name of a person, is capitalized when there is no possessive or article preceding it. Grandma and Mom went shopping. Grandma and my mom went shopping. | | | • | • | • | • |
| | **PUNCTUATION** | | | | | | | |
| 98 | **Periods: end of sentence** | Declarative sentences need a period at the end. | • | • | • | • | • | • |
| | **Period with abbreviation** | Mr. Jones; a.m. or p.m. | | | • | • | • | • |
| 100 | **Question marks: interrogative sentences** | Question marks are placed at the end of sentences that inquire. | • | • | • | • | • | • |
| 102 | **Exclamation points: exclamatory sentences and interjections** | An exclamation point is used for emphasis. Examples: Drip! Drop! I can't believe it is still raining! | • | • | • | • | • | • |
| 104 | **Commas: use in a series** | I need to buy shoes, socks, an umbrella, and a jacket. | | • | • | • | • | • |
| | **Comma to separate month, day, and year** | December 28, 2008 | | • | • | • | • | • |
| | **Comma to separate city and state** | Portland, Oregon | | • | • | • | • | • |
| | **Comma following a transition word at the beginning of sentences** | Finally, our long-awaited order arrived. | | • | • | • | • | • |
| | **Comma precedes a connecting word (coordinate conjunction) when combining two short sentences** | Anna has my library book, and Devon has my lunch. (Examples of connecting words: *so*, *or*, *but*, *and*) | | • | • | • | • | • |

| Page | Skill | Example | 1 | 2 | 3 | 4 | 5 | 6 |
|---|---|---|---|---|---|---|---|---|
| | **Comma with direct address** | Anna, grab your coat! | | | • | • | • | • |
| | **Commas in a letter** | Place a comma after the greeting and the closing. | | • | • | • | • | • |
| | **Comma surrounds an appositive** | Anna, the amazing runner, won the medal. | | | • | • | • | • |
| | **Comma: After an introductory phrase or clause** | When they heard the final bell, the children headed for the bus. | | | • | • | • | • |
| | **Comma to set off closer** | The children tiptoed down the hall, wondering what would happen next. | | | | | • | • |
| 106 | **Punctuation in dialogue** | "Hurry up!" cried Anna.<br>"Can you help me find my keys?" her mother asked. | • | • | • | • | • | • |
| 108 | **Apostrophes: contraction** | Can't, won't, shouldn't | • | • | • | • | • | • |
| 110 | **Apostrophes: Possessives** | Anna's bike is bright yellow. | • | • | • | • | • | • |
| | **Colon in reporting the time** | 10:30 a.m. | | | • | • | • | • |
| | **Colon at the beginning of a list** | They had a long list of errands, including the following: going to the grocery store, the post office, and the health food store. | | | • | • | • | • |
| | **Hyphen to join compound descriptions** | Heavy-handed dog trainer, father-in-law. | | | | • | • | • |
| | **Hyphen to separate syllables** | At the end of a line, if there isn't room for the entire word, syllables are separated by a hyphen. | | | | • | • | • |
| | **Underline or italicize a book title** | When a book play or title is handwritten, it should be underlined. | | | | • | • | • |
| | **Ellipses** | Use ellipses to indicate a pause in thought, or the omission of words or sentences. I won't go, but. . . | | | | • | • | • |

## SPELLING

| Page | Skill | Example | 1 | 2 | 3 | 4 | 5 | 6 |
|---|---|---|---|---|---|---|---|---|
| | **Spelling consciousness** | Students should have a high level of awareness that spelling is important. | • | • | • | • | • | • |
| 60 | **Stretching words** | Writers say words slowly to pull them apart auditorily. | • | • | • | • | • | • |

| | Skill | Description | | | | | | |
|---|---|---|---|---|---|---|---|---|
| 62 | **Reread to add more letters** | Rereading allows writers opportunities to modify spelling. | • | • | • | | | |
| 64 | **Big words have more letters than small words** | Writers need to expect to use more letters in longer words, as they develop spelling consciousness. | • | • | | | | |
| 70 | **Spelling reference: picture alphabet card** | Alphabet cards with picture cues help writers identify sound-symbol relationships. | • | • | | | | |
| 72 | **Spelling reference: class word wall** | Word walls help writers quickly access high-frequency words. Content word walls support spelling of content-specific words. | • | • | • | • | • | • |
| 74 | **Spelling reference: portable word wall** | Writers need a collection of alphabetized high-frequency words at their fingertips. | • | • | • | • | • | • |
| 66 | **Use known words to spell other words** | Spelling by analogy allows students to use known words and word parts to spell other words. If I can write *in*, then I can also write *pin*. | • | • | • | • | • | • |
| 68 | **Noticing syllables: each syllable needs a vowel** | Writers need to expect to place at least one vowel in every syllable. | • | • | • | • | • | • |
| | **Try different spellings for words** | When faced with an uncertain spelling, writers benefit from trying various spellings in the margin or on a separate sheet of paper. | | • | • | • | • | • |
| | **Homophones** | Homophones are words that sound the same but have different spellings and meanings (*their, there, they're*; *no, know*) | | • | • | • | • | • |
| **GRAMMAR** | | | | | | | | |
| 80 | **Complete sentences** | Writers avoid unintentional sentence fragments (T*he fuzzy puppy*) and need to acquire a strong foundation in writing complete, interesting sentences. (*The fuzzy puppy howled at the moon.*) | • | • | • | • | • | • |
| | **Phrase** | A phrase is a group of words that takes the place of a specific part of speech. *The house at the end of the street* is a phrase that acts like a noun. The phrase *at the end of the street* is a prepositional phrase that acts like an adjective. | | | • | • | • | • |
| | **Clause** | A clause is a word or group of words ordinarily consisting of a subject and a predicate. A clause usually contains a verb and may or may not be a sentence in its own right. (Example: I didn't know that the cat ran up the tree. *That the cat ran up the tree* is a clause. This clause includes the phrase *up the tree*.) | | | | • | • | • |

| | | | | | | | | |
|---|---|---|---|---|---|---|---|---|
| | **Sentence parts: simple subject and simple verb** | Writers understand the essential components of a sentence, the who or what does something (subject) and what the subject does (verb). Toddlers scamper. Brian cheered. | | • | • | • | • | • |
| | **Control sentence length vs. run-on sentences** | Writers use simple, compound, or complex sentences to enrich writing, while avoiding run-ons. Nonstandard: The fuzzy puppy snuggled in my arms and then he ate fast and played and barked and then he. . . Standard: The fuzzy puppy, while snuggling in my arms, fell quickly asleep. Then, he. . . | | • | • | • | • | • |
| 84 | **Using transition words** | Transition words are used to organize writing and alert readers to changes in the text. (Finally, our long-awaited order arrived.) | • | • | • | • | • | • |
| 86 | **Singular and plural nouns** | Writers understand the difference between singular and plural nouns, and can form plurals. | • | • | • | • | • | • |
| 82 | **Single vs. double subject** | Writers avoid the nonstandard double subject (My mom, she prefers. . .) and select single subjects for sentences (My mom prefers. . .). | • | • | • | • | • | • |
| 88 | **Singular subject-verb agreement** | A singular noun and pronoun (subject) agrees with its verb in number, case, and person. (Singular: Mary giggles.) | • | • | • | • | • | • |
| 90 | **Plural subject-verb agreement** | Plural nouns and pronouns (subjects) agree with their verbs in number, case, and person. (Plural: The babies wobble.) | • | • | • | • | • | • |
| 92 | **Past-tense verbs** | Writers differentiate between present- and past-tense verbs to show *when* an action takes place. (I sit on the edge of my bed. I sat on the edge of my bed.) | • | • | • | • | • | • |
| | **Verb tense: future** | Writers expand their use of verbs to show a future action or state of being. (Mario will be a stellar teacher.) | • | • | • | • | • | • |
| | **Verb types: action** | The most common verb is the action verb that tells what the subject is doing. (Mario swims across the lake.) | • | • | • | • | • | • |
| | **Verb types: linking** | Writers use linking verbs (nonaction verbs) to connect the subject with nouns, pronouns, or adjectives after the linking verbs *is*, *are*, *was*, *were*. (Margarita is my maternal aunt.) | • | • | • | • | • | • |
| | **Verb types: main** | When a verb is composed of two or more words, the verb at the end of the verb phrase is the main (principal) verb. (Anna is dancing down the hall.) | | | | • | • | • | • |
| | **Verb types: helping** | Writers use helping (auxiliary) verbs to create verb phrases that consist of a helping verb and the main (principal) verb. (Anna is dancing down the hall.) | | | | • | • | • | • |

| # | Skill | Description | | | | | | |
|---|---|---|---|---|---|---|---|---|
| | **Verb forms: regular** | Most verbs are regular. Writers add -ed to show a past action, or use a helping verb (has, had, have). | | | ● | ● | ● | ● |
| | **Verb forms: irregular** | Some verbs are irregular. Their past-tense form is not made by adding -ed or when using helping verbs. Past tense is expressed with a new word (run, ran). | | | ● | ● | ● | ● |
| 78 | **Pronoun order (person's name and then I, not me)** | Standard form: My mom and I. . . My mom, dad, and I. . . Nonstandard: Me and my mom. Me and my dad and my mom. . . | ● | ● | ● | ● | ● | ● |
| | **Pronouns and the nouns to which they refer (their antecedents)** | Writers identify the nouns to which pronouns refer. Standard: Niva is an exceptional cook. She whipped up dinner last night. Nonstandard: She is an exceptional cook. She whipped up dinner last night. | | ● | ● | ● | ● | ● |
| 94 | **Possessive pronouns** | Possessive pronouns take the place of a noun and show ownership. Most possessive pronouns are written without an apostrophe (my, our, their). | ● | ● | ● | ● | ● | ● |
| | **Subjective and objective cases of pronouns and nouns** | Nouns remain the same for both subjective and objective cases, whereas pronouns require differentiation between the subjective (I, you, he, she, it, we, you, they) and objective (me, you, him, her, it, us, you, them) cases. | | | | ● | ● | ● |
| | **Double negatives** | Only one word should be used to express a negative idea. Frequent errors occur when writers use not with never, no, hardly, and so on. Standard: We don't have any paper towels. Nonstandard: We don't got no paper towels. | | | | ● | ● | ● |
| | **Adjectives: To lift description** | Writers include adjectives, words that describe nouns and pronouns, to strengthen text. (The brilliant butterfly zipped past the decrepit barn.) | ● | ● | ● | ● | ● | ● |
| | **Adjectives: comparative and superlative forms** | Adjectives can be used to compare two or more people, places, things, or ideas. (Examples: bigger, biggest; more/less helpful; most/least helpful) | | | ● | ● | ● | ● |
| | **Articles** | Articles are adjectives. The indicates a specific (definite) article. (Bring me the striped sweater.) A and an refer to no particular thing. A is used before a consonant sound. (Bring me a sweater.) An is used before a vowel sound. (Bring me an apple.) | | ● | ● | ● | ● | ● |
| | **Adverbs and adverb phrases** | Adverbs modify verbs, adjectives, or other adverbs. Most adverbs tell when, where, how, and to what extent/degree. (Marcos quickly zipped over the goal line.) | | | ● | ● | ● | ● |
| | **Adverbs: comparative and superlative forms** | Adverbs can be used to compare two or more people, places, things, or ideas. (Examples: faster, fastest; more/less carefully; most/least carefully) | | | | ● | ● | ● |

| | | | | | | | | |
|---|---|---|---|---|---|---|---|---|
| 102 | **Interjections** | Interjections are words or phrases that are used to express a strong emotion and are separated from the rest of the sentence by a comma or an exclamation point. (Wow! This is cool! Wow, this is cool!) | • | • | • | • | • | • |
| | **Prepositions and prepositional phrases** | Prepositions are not modifiers; their function is to relate a noun or pronoun to another word in the sentence. A prepositional phrase includes a preposition, the object of the preposition, and any modifiers. (The cat snoozed under the lawn chair.) | | | • | • | • | • |
| | **Conjunctions: coordinate** | Conjunctions connect words or groups of words. Coordinate conjunctions connect equal parts: words, phrases, and independent clauses (sentences). (Examples of coordinating conjunctions: for, and, nor, but, or, yet, so) | • | • | • | • | • | |
| | **Conjunctions: subordinate** | Conjunctions connect words or groups of words. Subordinate conjunctions connect two clauses to make complex sentences. (Examples of subordinating conjunctions: after, because, before, until, when, while) | | | • | • | • | • |

# PART III

**Rereading for multiple purposes helps writers look closely at meaning and conventions.**

# Lesson Cycles for Mastering the Mechanics

## Cycles for Understanding the Editing Process

**W**riters need to consider mechanics and conventions as tools to lift their messages, clarify meaning, and focus their editing as they prepare for an audience.

Rereading is a tool that engages writers in processing print while supporting them at every phase of the drafting and editing processes. It is, unquestionably, our greatest tool for supporting the editing process.

- Writers need to reread constantly. They reread to confirm their message, regain momentum, and consider what to say next. They reread to think about letters, sounds, and word choice. They reread to edit or to make sure they have placed their name on the paper.

- Editing checklists guide writers in rereading for conventions and mechanics.

- Focused edits engage writers in a process of rereading once for each editing point.

# Putting Your Name on the Paper

**DAY 1**  **Model the Focus Point**

Note: Create a card with your name on it to use during modeling and post a piece of writing and drawing that you have created in advance.

**Modeled Writing Sample**

Fast-Flying Bird

By Mrs. Smith

Screetch! Screetch! The big bird was diving out of the sky. Vroom! Vroom! That bird can really fly!

> **I want anyone who reads my writing or looks at my drawings to know that they are mine, so I always write my name on my paper. If I didn't know how to write my name, I could look at my name card to help me. Watch me write my name on my paper. First things first!**

Write your name on your paper, using your name card to check the spelling and letter formation. Go back to reread, touch, and spell the letters in your name. Add a few words to your draft or add labels to your drawing so children see that writing the author's name is part of the drafting/editing process.)

 **TURN AND TALK** Writers, talk about putting your name on your writing. What did you see me doing? What will you need to do every time you write?

 **SUM IT UP** Now that I have finished writing for today, notice how I think like an editor and go back to check my work. I know writers put their names on their papers. I am first going to reread to be sure I made sense, and then I will check to be sure my name is there. I will use my name card to be sure I didn't leave out any letters.

**DAY 2**  **Guided Practice**

Place a piece of student writing on the overhead projector, using either an example from your class or the sample on appendix page 172. If the author is one of your students, invite the author to read the selection to the class.

 **TURN AND TALK**

- Writers, think together about a celebration we can offer this author. What can you say about the meaning? What did the author do well?

- We have been working on writing our name on the page. Think together: Did the author remember to write his or her name on the paper?

 **SUM IT UP** To a class editing chart, add "Write your name on your paper."

Remember, writers, authors need to put a name on their work.

Model how to review papers in a writing folder to look for a name on each piece. Ask your writers to look at their writing folders and select a few pieces of writing; then give them a few minutes to look at their work to check that their names are on their papers.

 **PEER EDIT** Show your partner where you put your name on your papers. Show your partner if you found a page where you forgot! Think together about your writing.

 **SUM IT UP** Remember, the first thing writers do is put their names on their papers. I am going to ask you to work with a partner and look at books you have in your independent reading collection and in our classroom library. With each book, look together to find the place where the author put his or her name.

 **Assess the Learning**

- Use a class record-keeping grid as you observe editors at work. Check off those students who are writing their names at the top of the paper without being prompted.

- Confer with individual writers to go through writing folders, checking for places where their names have or have not been added.

## Link the Learning

- Those students who do not yet place their names on their work can be gathered into a brief guided writing experience in which you might again model how writers put their names on their papers right off the bat!

- During writer's workshop, remind students to write their names on their papers before they do anything else.

- In all content areas, have learners do "first things first" by writing their names on their papers.

- Examine big books, classroom charts, poetry posters, and other familiar texts to ensure that the name of the author is written clearly.

- Show students several examples of writing from classroom authors and library books. Compare the places where authors choose to put their names.

# Counting the Words in a Message

**DAY 1** | **Model the Focus Point**

As you begin writing in front of the students, your think-aloud might sound something like the following:

> I am going to write about the pizza I had for lunch today. It was yummy. I think I will make that my first sentence: *The pizza at lunch was really yummy.* I am going to say the sentence again so I can count the words in the sentence. Watch me hold up one finger for each word I say. Ready: *The... pizza... at... lunch... was... really... yummy.* Wow! I am holding up seven fingers because there are seven words in my sentence. Let's do it together. Hold up one finger for each word. Watch, I am going to write seven words and put a space between each word.

**Modeled Writing Sample**

Yummy Pizza

By _____

The pizza at lunch was really yummy. The cheese melted and covered the whole crust. My favorite topping is pepperoni!

As you add each word, keep returning to the beginning of the sentence to count words and reread. When you finish, have students read the sentence with you twice, once to make sure it makes sense, and then to count the words one last time. If time allows, add a second sentence.

**TURN AND TALK** Writers, use your fingers and count out the words in my sentence. Share your thinking about how I helped myself remember all the words.

**SUM IT UP** Writers can count the words in their sentences before they begin writing, to help them remember the words they want to write. The number of words they say needs to match the number of words that they write.

**DAY 2** | **Guided Practice**

Place a piece of student writing on the overhead projector or use the sample on appendix page 173. If the author is one of your students, invite the author to read the selection to the class.

**TURN AND TALK**

- Partners, talk together about a celebration you can offer the author. What can you say about the meaning? What did the author do well?

- Our editing focus has been on counting the words to be sure we wrote all the words we think we wrote. Writers, work together to count the number of words in the first sentence. Do you think the writer left out any words? How can you tell?

The moon sion on the Earth

If students have suggestions for changes to the piece, ask permission from the author before executing the changes.

**SUM IT UP** To a class editing chart, add "Count the words in each sentence."

**Remember, writers can help themselves by counting the words in their sentences as they write.**

## DAY 3  Independent Practice

Show writers how to go through a writing folder and select a piece to reread. Model counting the words and thinking about possible omissions. Add missing words that you may notice. Ask writers to look through their own writing folders and select a piece of writing. Their goal is to count the words in their sentences and determine if they have omitted any words. Did they find a place where counting the words in their sentence(s) helped them decide if they needed to add another word?

 **PEER EDIT** Share with your partner what you noticed about the number of words in your sentence. Did the number of words you counted match the number of words that you had written? Share your thinking about using spaces. How did you do?

 **SUM IT UP** Writers can count the words in their sentences before they begin writing so they remember all the words they want to write. The number of words on the paper needs to match the words in a sentence.

### ✓ Assess the Learning

- Use a class record-keeping grid as you observe editors at work. Check off those students who count out the words in their sentences before they write.

- Meet with writers individually to have them generate sentences orally and count the number of words.

### ∞ Link the Learning

- During writer's workshop, remind writers to count out the words before they begin writing.

- Read selected sentences from familiar big books and picture books. Have children repeat the sentence and count the words.

- Provide additional modeled writings in which you say a sentence and count the words on your fingers before writing.

- During shared writing or interactive writing, have students count words before beginning to write.

# Reread and Touch Each Word

## DAY 1 — Model the Focus Point

I want the words I write to match the words I say. Good writers get their ideas on the paper, and then they reread and check to make sure all the words are on the paper. When I write, I put my ideas down quickly. Then I reread to make sure it says what I think it does. Watch me. First, I will write. Then, I will reread to be sure this makes sense. Finally, I will reread and <u>touch</u> each word as I read it. I want to make sure that I didn't leave out any of my words.

 **TURN AND TALK** Writers, talk about the way I reread my writing. What did you see me doing? What did you hear me doing? Why was I doing all of that?

 **SUM IT UP** Remember, authors get their ideas on the paper first. Then, after writing, they reread and touch each word to make sure they didn't leave out any words. Authors know that they want their talking and the words on the page to match.

---

**Modeled Writing Sample**

Better Than a Fork!

By Mr. Allen

I'm glad that there are spoons. It would take way too long to eat soup with a fork. I wonder who invented spoons anyway?

---

## DAY 2 — Guided Practice

Place a piece of student writing on the overhead projector. Use either a writing sample from your class or the sample from appendix page 186. If the author is one of your students, invite the author to read the selection to the class.

**TURN AND TALK**

• Writers, talk about a celebration you can offer this author. What can you say about the meaning? What did the author do well?

• Think together. How should the author check for missing words? What should happen after the ideas are on the paper?

If there are suggestions for changes, ask permission from the author before writing on the piece.

 **SUM IT UP** To a class editing chart, add "Reread: Touch each word."

Remember, writers, this is an editing strategy that helps writers catch missed words.

Demonstrate going through a writing folder and selecting a piece to reread. Model touching each word carefully and then adding a word that was missed. Ask the writers to look at their own writing folders and select a piece of writing to reread. Remind them to touch each word as they reread and add words if they need to.

 **PEER EDIT** Use a piece of writing to show your partner how you can touch each word as you reread. Share any words you were able to add when you reread.

**SUM IT UP** Remember, writers, first you get your ideas on the page and then you reread. The idea is to reread and touch each word to make sure that you didn't leave out any words.

## ✔ Assess the Learning

- Use a class record-keeping grid as you observe editors at work. Check off those students who are touching the words as they reread to make sure they didn't omit any words.

- Circulate and ask each student to reread his or her writing, touching each word during the reread.

## Link the Learning

- During writer's workshop, remind students to touch each word as they reread their writing.

- Those who are not rereading and touching words can be gathered into a brief guided writing experience where you might again model rereading and touching each word.

- During shared reading of a poem, use a pointer to model how you touch below each word as you read, to make sure that you don't leave out any words.

- After multiple shared reading interactions with the same poem, provide individual poetry pages for choral reading. Have students practice touching each word as they read.

# Focused Edit: Reread for Each Editing Point

## DAY 1 — Model the Focus Point

Writers, we have learned how important it is to reread our writing. We all need to remember that writers don't reread just once. They reread for each editing point. I am going to read through this once and touch each word to make sure I have all the words I need. Watch now as I start at the beginning, one more time, and think about spaces between my words. For my third rereading, I am going to think about spelling. By thinking about only one thing each time I reread, I can do a better job of editing!

 **TURN AND TALK** Writers, what did you notice about the way I reread my writing? What were the reasons I reread? Why shouldn't I try to check for everything on the list all at once?

 **SUM IT UP** Writers reread many times, focusing on just one thing at a time.

> **Modeled Writing Sample**
>
> Ice Cream Cone
>
> Colorful scoops of flavor
>
> Perched on a crunchy cone
>
> Tongue dashes out
>
> Mmmmm
>
> Love those drips!

## DAY 2 — Guided Practice

Place a piece of student writing on the overhead projector. Use a sample from a student in class or appendix page 175. If the author is one of your students, invite the author to read the selection to the class.

**TURN AND TALK**

- Writers, talk about a celebration you can offer the author. What can you say about the meaning? What did the author do well?

- Let's look at our class editing chart and decide how many times we will reread this writing. Remember, we check for one thing each time we reread.

**SUM IT UP** To a class editing chart, add "Reread for each editing point."

When we have our conferences to talk about writing, be ready to tell me how many times you reread and what you were checking for each time.

**DAY 3** | **Independent Practice**

Model how to select a piece of writing from a writing folder, and then go to the class editing chart. Think aloud as you review the chart, identify the reasons you have for rereading, and count the number of rereads you will be doing. Have students select a piece of writing from their folders, identify purposes for rereading, and then reread once for each purpose.

 **PEER EDIT** Partners, show each other the way you reread for each editing point. Point out anything you were able to change during your rereading. Think together!

 **SUM IT UP** Writers reread a lot, but they are careful to look for only one thing each time they reread their work.

 **Assess the Learning**

- While conferring with writers, assess their ability to reread multiple times for multiple purposes.
- Meet with small groups of editors as they reread for multiple purposes. Identify those who would benefit from more modeling

**Link the Learning**

- Using a selected page from a big book, reread several times, modeling how to check for a different editing focus on each successive reading.
- Gather a guided writing group of those students who need more support in rereading for specific purposes.
- Gather literature selections such as *Farmer Duck, Are You My Mother? Where's Spot*, and *Don't Let the Pigeon Drive the Bus*. Review each title once and count only periods. Review again and count only question marks. Review a third time for a different purpose. Create a chart showing the counts from each reread.
- Have writers select another writing selection to proofread. Be sure they reread for each editing point.
- Have partners edit together, rereading for a variety of focus points. Encourage them to share their discoveries.

# Using an Editing Checklist

## DAY 1 — Model the Focus Point

Note: Prepare the writing in advance.

**Writers do many things to make it easier for people to read their writing. Just like a gardener uses a rake to tidy up the lawn, a writer can use an editing checklist to tidy up his or her writing. Here are the steps writers follow: A writer gets ideas on paper and then rereads the writing to be sure it makes sense. After that, writers sometimes use an editing checklist. Watch me. I am going to read carefully and check for every item on my checklist.**

 **TURN AND TALK Writers, what did you notice about the way I used the editing checklist? How many times did you hear me reread my writing? Why shouldn't I try to check for everything on the list all at once?**

**SUM IT UP When writers finish their writing, they can use an editing checklist to help make the writing easy for others to read.**

> **Modeled Writing Sample**
>
> Swish
>
> By Mrs. T
>
> Yellow races around her fishbowl, streaking through the water with a flash of gold. I am so lucky to have a great fish like her.

## DAY 2 — Guided Practice

Place a piece of student writing on the overhead projector. Use a sample from a student in class or use appendix page 176. If the author is one of your students, invite the author to read the selection to the class.

**TURN AND TALK**

- **Writers, talk about a celebration you can offer the author. What can you say about the meaning? What did the author do well?**

- **Let's use an editing checklist and reread for each item we are going to check in the writing. If we have three items on our list, how many times will we reread the writing?**

**SUM IT UP** To a class editing chart, add "Use an editing checklist to double-check your writing."

**Writers, authors use editing checklists to help them remember what to look for when they reread and get a piece ready to share with others.**

**DAY 3** | **Independent Practice**

Model how to lay out a piece of writing with your editing checklist. Think out loud about how you use an editing checklist only when all the ideas in the writing are on the paper; then show how to reread for each item on the list. Ask writers to select a piece of writing and use the editing checklist, copied from appendix pages 165 and 166, to support proofreading.

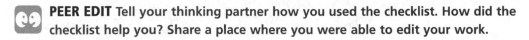 **PEER EDIT** Tell your thinking partner how you used the checklist. How did the checklist help you? Share a place where you were able to edit your work.

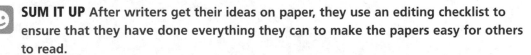 **SUM IT UP** After writers get their ideas on paper, they use an editing checklist to ensure that they have done everything they can to make the papers easy for others to read.

## ✅ Assess the Learning

• Use a class record-keeping grid as you observe editors at work. Check off those students who are able to use the editing checklist.

• Meet with small groups of editors as they use their checklists, to assess their ability to use the list independently.

## ∞ Link the Learning

• During writer's workshop, remind writers to use an editing checklist. (Reteaching may be needed.)

• Gather a guided writing group of those students who need more support in using a checklist.

• Model writing and rereading with a checklist, using multiple writing selections so students can see that you use checklists on a wide variety of writing samples.

• Have writers select another writing selection to proofread. Be sure they reread for each editing point.

• Have partners use checklists and edit together, rereading for each focus point. Encourage them to share their discoveries.

# Cycles for Utilizing Space on the Page

**E**mergent learners are often challenged by the space on a page and how to use it. They are often unsure about how far across the page to carry their text, how to use the margin, and how to cluster letters together so readers can tell the words apart.

To assist children with understanding the proper use of space in their writing, we believe it is essential to highlight the way published authors have used space in picture books and enlarged texts. We also need to think aloud about space on the page as we craft modeled writing in front of children. Hearing us talk about using up an entire line before moving to the next, saving room for a second picture, or writing a poem that has a long, narrow shape will help children see that space is one of the tools we use as writers.

With the guidance of much-loved stories and a teacher who thinks aloud explicitly about spaces on a page, young learners quickly begin to see their options for space, print, and visuals.

One of our greatest wishes is to expose our youngest children to writing and drawing that continues over several pages, with page numbers and connected thinking. Kindergarten and first-grade students must understand that their writing, like that of published authors, is worthy of many pages on the same topic.

# Word Boundaries: Keep Letters in a Word Close Together

## DAY 1 — Model the Focus Point

Note: If you have a whiteboard available, you can use it to model both correct and incorrect spacing of letters and word boundaries.

> **Words are made up of letters, so when I write, I need to think about the sounds in each word, but I also have to think about spacing. As I write, I'll talk to you about what I'm thinking. I need to help my reader see which letters go together to make a word. I also need to be sure I have left spaces between words so each word is separated. I am writing the word *pop*. Notice how the letters, *p-o-p*, are close together. That tells my reader that this is one word. Now, watch me leave a space before I start the next word. Do you see how I keep all the letters in a word close together? When I finish my message, I will reread to be sure it makes sense. Then I will reread again to make sure that all the letters in a word are close together and that there are spaces between my words.**

 **TURN AND TALK** Writers, talk about what you saw me doing as I wrote. What did you notice about my spacing?

**SUM IT UP** Writers, letters in a word need to be right next to each other so we can tell that they belong together. We also need spaces between each word so we can tell where one word stops and the next one begins.

---

**Modeled Writing Sample**

**Popcorn**

By Mrs. H

The microwave is running and soon I will have buttery popcorn crunching in my mouth. Pop! Pop! Poppety-pop!

---

## DAY 2 — Guided Practice

Place a piece of student writing on the overhead projector. Use either the writing sample from appendix page 177 or one from your class. If the author is one of your students, invite the author to read the selection to the class.

 **TURN AND TALK**

- Writers, talk about a celebration you can offer the author. What can you say about the meaning of the selection? Let's compliment this author.

- Now, think together about spacing. Are the letters in each word right next to each other? Is there a space between each word?

If students have suggestions, ask permission from the author before executing the changes.

**SUM IT UP** To a class editing chart, add "Keep letters in a word close together."

Remember, writers always keep letters in a word right next to each other and leave spaces between the words.

### DAY 3 Independent Practice

Use a writing folder and model how to select a piece of writing and reread it to edit. Show students how you first check for meaning. Then, reread to see if letters in a word are close together. Ask writers to look in their writing folders, select a piece of writing, and check to see if the letters in each word are close together. Are there spaces between words?

 **PEER EDIT** Show your partner a place where the letters in a word are right next to each other in your writing. Be sure to show your partner where you remembered to put spaces between words, too. Show each other where you need to add a space or move the letters closer together.

 **SUM IT UP** Remember, writers know that letters in a word need to be right next to each other. Writers also put spaces between words so they can see where each word begins.

### ✔ Assess the Learning

- Use a class record-keeping grid as you observe editors at work. Use two columns: one to check off those students who put letters in a word close together, and the second to identify those who leave a space between words.

- During small-group instruction, have students frame individual words. Assess to see which students can identify word boundaries in print.

### 🔗 Link the Learning

- During writer's workshop, remind students to write letters in a word close together and then leave a space before beginning to write the next word.

- Gather students who need extra work on spacing for an interactive write, to guide them as they write letters in a word close together and then leave a space.

- During shared reading, point out the spaces between words and the clusters of letters that differentiate one word from another.

- During independent reading, have students pay attention to the spaces between words and notice the way letters are clustered together. Provide an opportunity for them to share their observations.

# Using the Entire Page

I want to write about a pond where I had the chance to see lots of ducks. As I get ready to write, I need to think about how I will use the piece of paper. When I look at my favorite books, I notice that the authors use the whole page. I am going to do that, too. I will place my picture at the top, and then I want to be sure that my words fill the paper all the way across the page as well as down to the bottom. Do you see how my words fill the entire line before I move down to the next line of writing? When I finish writing, notice how I reread at least two times. I will read once to be sure I made sense, and then again to think about how well I did at using the whole page.

> **Modeled Writing Sample**
>
> Ducks at the Pond
>
> The sun was shining and I could hear ducks quacking as we walked along the path. Some of the ducks were upside down with their tail feathers in the air as they searched for their dinner.

 **TURN AND TALK** How did I do at using the whole page? Did each line go all the way across before I started a new line? Did I keep going to the bottom of the page? What do you think of where I placed my picture? Could I have put it somewhere else?

**SUM IT UP** Writers have to think about meaning, but they also have to think about how they are using the page. Remember, writers, begin writing on the top left and write all the way across the page before moving to the next line.

**DAY 2** **Guided Practice**

Place a piece of student writing on the overhead projector. Select a writing sample that will generate conversation about carrying words out to the margin and using the entire page. You may want to consider the sample on appendix page 172. If the author is one of your students, invite the author to read the selection to the class.

 **TURN AND TALK**

- Partners, talk together about a celebration you can offer the author. What can you say about the meaning of the selection? Give compliments about the writing.

- Think together about how this author used the page. Did the author use the whole page? What do you notice?

If students have suggestions for changes, ask permission from the author before executing the changes.

**SUM IT UP** To a class editing chart, add "Use the entire page."

Writers, it is important to remember that writers have to think about their message and about how they will use the page. Writing needs to go all the way across before moving to a new line. Writers are careful about how they use the space on their page.

## DAY 3 | Independent Practice

Model looking through a writing folder and thinking out loud about using the entire page. Share your thinking about filling each line before moving to the next, placing illustrations in interesting places and trying to make writing look like pages in published books. Ask writers to look in their writing folders and think about how they used their pages. Ask them to see if they started writing on the top left, wrote across the page, and used a return sweep with spaces between words. Did they remember to use the whole line before transitioning to a new line?

 **PEER EDIT** Check each other's papers and share what you noticed. Did the first word begin at the top-left part of the paper? Are the words written all the way across the paper? Did your partner use a return sweep back to the left-hand side of the paper? Where is the illustration? Is there anywhere else it could have been placed? Think together.

 **SUM IT UP** Remember, writers plan how to use all the space on the page.

### ✅ Assess the Learning

- Use a Class Record-Keeping Grid (see appendix page 170) as you observe editors at work. Identify students who may need another lesson on using the entire page.

- Meet with individual writers to confer about use of a page. Assess understanding of directionality, margins, return sweep, and flexibility of placement for an illustration.

### ⚭ Link the Learning

- During writer's workshop, remind writers to write from top to bottom, left to right, using return sweep and spaces between words. Help them apply what they know as they craft writing selections.

- Help children examine the use of space in picture books and enlarged texts. Show them how the author wrote across the entire line before sweeping to the next line.

- Model placing visuals, showing children different placements for the illustration, and how you can move the text to complement the picture placement.

- During small-group instruction, guide conversations about using an entire line, return sweep, placement of illustration, and so on.

# Using Multiple Pages

**Model the Focus Point**

Before the lesson, arrange three large sheets of paper, side by side, in a place where students can easily see them.

**Page 1**

An ant is a tiny insect that lives in a burrow.

**Page 2**

An ant has feelers on its head.

**Page 3**

Ants have six legs.

When authors create books, they use lots of pages. I have placed three sheets of paper on the wall because I am going to write at least three pages to make a book about ants. Watch as I quickly place one ant fact and an illustration on each page. I am not coloring my illustrations right now. I will make quick sketches to help me remember what goes on each page. Listen to me think out loud as I write. Then listen as I plan for more pages. When I finish three pages, I will stop and reread to edit. I need to reread and see if it makes sense. Good editors reread a lot. On another day, I might add more pages and work on my illustrations. I bet I can make a really long book if I keep going!

 **TURN AND TALK** Writers, talk together. Writing lots of pages on the same topic is fun. If I keep going, what else could I say about ants? Did you notice my page numbers? How do those help me as a writer? Think like editors. What do you notice when you reread?

**SUM IT UP** The books we read have many pages. As writers, we need to think about the ways we can use multiple pages to share our thinking. Writers, you can write books!

**DAY 2** **Guided Practice**

Place multiple-page student writing from the appendix, page 185, on the overhead. Engage children in a conversation about the writing and how everyone can plan and write multiple-page pieces.

 **TURN AND TALK**
- Writers, talk about a celebration you can offer the author. What can you say about the meaning of the selection? What do you notice about the number of pages? Give compliments about the writing.

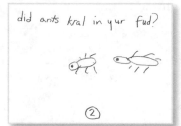

- **Now, think together. Could the one page of writing turn into lots of pages? What do we know about writing books with lots of pages?**

If students have suggestions, ask permission from the author before executing the changes.

 **SUM IT UP** To a class editing chart, add "Writers can use multiple pages."

**Writers, you are ready to write books. When you plan your writing, think about the number of pages you want to use. Using several pages for writing is one way in which to write more and share your thinking.**

## DAY 3 | Independent Practice

Model taking a writing folder and rereading a few pieces to think about turning the writing into multiple pages. Think aloud about additional ideas for the topic, the contents of each page, pictures to capture the idea for each page, and so on. Ask writers to look in their writing folders and select a piece of writing that could be extended. Encourage the sharing of ideas about pieces that could be extended, and what would go on the additional pages.

 **PEER EDIT Show your partner your writing. If you wrote a book, share some of the pages. If you wrote a single page, share your plan for turning it into a book. Think together.**

 **SUM IT UP Let's look at one of our favorite big books and count the pages. Let's see how many pages this author wrote. Wow! Writers use lots of pages with pictures and words to share their thinking. They use page numbers and titles, and for sure, they add their names to their work. This is what good writers and good editors do.**

##  Assess the Learning

- Identify students who are still confused about multiple-page writing experiences, and gather them into a small group for another modeled write of a multiple-page book. Show them that a book can be just pictures and page numbers before words are added. Assess understanding.

- Gather writers in small groups to share their multiple-page writing selections, and assess their understanding of how to implement and edit a multiple-page piece.

##  Link the Learning

- Create multiple-page books as retellings of favorite stories, nonfiction summaries, or personal narratives. Be sure to add page numbers, a title, and a cover.

- Write and edit alphabet books as another way to extend thinking about multiple-page books.

- During small-group instruction, take time to count pages and talk about the pages this author chose to use in sharing his or her thinking.

# Cycles for Moving Forward With Spelling

It has been well proven that spelling ability is developmental and that it goes hand-in-hand with print knowledge in reading and in writing. In addition to print knowledge, children need to have *strategies* for navigating the challenges of crafting letters and sounds into meaningful print. When they approach spelling tasks strategically, they have a sense of when to rely upon themselves and their own knowledge of letters and sounds and when to go to the word wall or to a personal resource, such as an picture alphabet card. Because strategic spellers know how to navigate their work in word building, they pay attention to the way words look, and may notice patterns in words. Strategic spellers have a distinct sense of *spelling consciousness* that guides them in their writing.

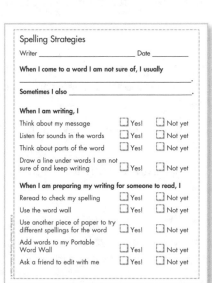

Spelling Strategies

Writer _____ Date _____

When I come to a word I am not sure of, I usually
_____.

Sometimes I also _____.

When I am writing, I

| | | |
|---|---|---|
| Think about my message | ☐ Yes! | ☐ Not yet |
| Listen for sounds in the words | ☐ Yes! | ☐ Not yet |
| Think about parts of the word | ☐ Yes! | ☐ Not yet |
| Draw a line under words I am not sure of and keep writing | ☐ Yes! | ☐ Not yet |

When I am preparing my writing for someone to read, I

| | | |
|---|---|---|
| Reread to check my spelling | ☐ Yes! | ☐ Not yet |
| Use the word wall | ☐ Yes! | ☐ Not yet |
| Use another piece of paper to try different spellings for the word | ☐ Yes! | ☐ Not yet |
| Add words to my Portable Word Wall | ☐ Yes! | ☐ Not yet |
| Ask a friend to edit with me | ☐ Yes! | ☐ Not yet |

# Stretching Words

**DAY 1** | **Model the Focus Point**

Writers, we are going to practice stretching out words and listening to the sounds. That is one of the most helpful things writers do. I've decided to write about a time when I was your age and I got in trouble for talking when we were supposed to be quiet while standing in line. Watch how I stretch out the words and write the sounds I hear. *I got in trouble. I g-o-t. . .* I hear *g* and *t*, so I will write those sounds. *In. . .* I hear *i-n*. (Continue writing as you demonstrate saying words slowly and writing sounds. Be sure to emphasize initial and final sounds—the easiest sounds.) **When I write the sounds I hear, it helps me get my ideas written more quickly so I don't forget what I am trying to say!**

> **Modeled Writing Sample**
>
> **Oops**
>
> By Mrs. T
>
> I gt in trbl fr tkg in lin. I hd to go to the nd ov the lin.
>
> I wz mbrsst.
>
> (I got in trouble for talking in line. I had to go to the end of the line. I was embarrassed.)

 **TURN AND TALK** Writers, tell each other what I did to help myself spell and write. What did you see me doing with the words? What did you notice as I stretched out my words?

 **SUM IT UP** Remember, writers stretch out words and write down the letters they hear. They don't have to spell every word perfectly at first.

**DAY 2** | **Guided Practice**

Place an example of student writing on the overhead projector, using either a sample from your class or appendix page 175. If the author is one of your students, invite the author to read the selection to the class.

 **TURN AND TALK**

• Writers, talk about a celebration you can offer the author. What can you say about the meaning of the selection? Give compliments about the writing.

• Think together. What do you notice about the way the author stretched out words?

If students have suggestions for changes, ask permission from the author before executing the changes.

 **SUM IT UP** To a class editing chart, add "Stretch words to hear sounds."

Writers, we know how to say words slowly, to stretch them out and listen to the sounds. This will help us write more and get our ideas on paper!

**DAY 3** | **Independent Practice**

Use a previously created modeled writing to demonstrate looking through your writing and thinking about stretching out more words. Demonstrate how you can add letters to a paper, even though it wasn't written today. Ask the writers to look in their writing folders and select a piece of writing that was completed earlier, to see if they can stretch out some words and add more letters.

 **PEER EDIT** Tell your partner what you did to help yourself spell your words. Share places where you stretched words and added more letters to your words.

 **SUM IT UP** Remember, writers use their ears. They say words slowly and listen to the sounds!

 **Assess the Learning**

- As writers are working, circulate and listen to them stretch out words. Gather data showing children who use this strategy and those who would benefit from additional small-group support.

- Have writers circle a few words that they stretched out in their writing. Record anecdotal notes about their understandings.

 **Link the Learning**

- During writer's workshop remind writers to stretch words and write the letters or chunks they know. Model with individuals as they work to stretch words and listen to the sounds.

- Encourage children to stretch words while writing lists, directions, invitations, recipes, notes, labels, poetry, math or science journals, and so on.

- Model stretching and writing words for signs in the classroom, poetry charts, lists of center activities, and other environmental print sources.

- During small-group instruction, guide children in stretching out words that appear in the leveled reading selections. Then have them write about their reading, stretching words as they draft their writing.

- After a shared reading, identify several key words from the selection that you will have everyone stretch and write. If whiteboards are available, have children write on them and share with partners the sounds they can identify.

- Gather children who can already stretch and spell short words, and model how to chunk words and insert known chunks into their writing.

# Reread to Add More Letters

## DAY 1 | Model the Focus Point

In advance, prepare a piece of writing in which you have used temporary spelling.

> We know writers stretch out words and write the sounds they know. But here is another important job for writers: Reread to see if you can think of more letters to add. My first sentence is *Fall is my favorite season*. As I touch each word and think about letters I know, I am thinking of letters to add! Look at the word *favit*. As I reread, I am hearing *or* in the middle of that word. I am going to add an *r* so the word will have more of the sounds I can hear. I can add letters to *seez* too. I hear an *n* at the end. I am going to add an *n* so it says, *seezn*. Rereading is helping me add letters!

> **Modeled Writing Sample**
>
> Fall
>
> Fl is my favit seez. I lik it becuz of all the butfl clrs in the leaves. Brit ylo is the bst of al the clrs.

 **TURN AND TALK** Think together about what you saw me doing as I added more letters. What did you hear me doing? How will rereading help you add more letters to your words?

 **SUM IT UP** Remember, writers reread their writing to see if they can add more letters.

## DAY 2 | Guided Practice

Guide children in examining a writing sample from appendix page 177 or from your class. If the author is one of your students, invite the author to read the selection to the class.

 **TURN AND TALK**

- Writers, talk about a celebration you can offer the author. What can you say about the meaning of the selection? Give compliments about the writing.

- Think together. Stretch out the words with your partner. Do you hear the same sounds the author heard? Can you think of any letters to add?

 **SUM IT UP** To a class editing chart, add "Reread writing to add letters."

Remember, writers, this is an editing strategy we will all use.

My dog sleeps with me in my bed every night I love my dog

Danny

**DAY 3** **Independent Practice**

Ask writers to look through their writing folders and select a piece of writing to reread. Give them a few minutes to look at their work and attempt to add more letters.

 **PEER EDIT** Partners, share the way you reread and tried to add letters. Read your work together and help each other add letters.

 **SUM IT UP** Remember, writers reread their writing to look at the words and add more letters.

## ✔ Assess the Learning

- Use a class record-keeping grid as you observe editors at work. Check off those students who are rereading and adding more letters.

- Confer with individuals to assess their ability to reread and add letters.

## 🔗 Link the Learning

- During writer's workshop, remind students to reread their writing for missing letters.

- Model writing lists, notes, and other functional texts, making sure to reread and add letters with each example.

- Encourage writers to write captions to accompany paintings or other artistic creations. Assist them in remembering to reread and add all the letters they can.

- Select a familiar big book and use slim strips of sticky notes to mask off beginning sounds and word endings from selected words. Have children read the text with you and try to identify the missing letters.

- After multiple shared reading interactions with the same text, provide partners with a portion of the text that has been retyped with missing letters. Have them locate the omissions and edit.

# Big Words Have More Letters Than Small Words

**DAY 1**  **Model the Focus Point**

One of the tricks writers learn is to think about words that are big and words that are small. Writers know big words have more letters than small words. Let's practice: Let's try *it* and *soccer*. Which one is the big word? Which one will have more letters? I can even count the sounds so I know about how many letters to write. Listen: In the word, *it*, I hear *i-t,* so I know I need to write two letters. In *soccer*, I hear *s-o-c-r*. Use your fingers. How many sounds are in that word?

> **Modeled Writing Sample**
>
> Racing down the soccer field with my team is fun. I even scored a goal!

Begin drafting and think aloud about big words and small words as you complete your writing.

 **TURN AND TALK** Writers, talk to each other about the difference between spelling bigger words and spelling smaller words. What did you see me doing? What did you hear me doing?

 **SUM IT UP** Writers, remember that big words have more letters than small words.

**DAY 2**  **Guided Practice**

Select a writing sample from a student in your class or use samples on appendix page 187. Place the writing on a transparency. If the author is one of your students, invite the author to read the selection to the class.

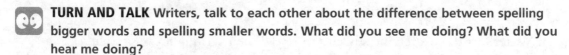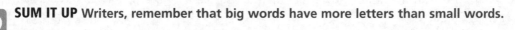

| From the desk of | From the desk of |
|---|---|
| KEEGAN | ANDY |
| I LIKmI  AR | Git sm |
| HKe TABL | +0f PAST |

**TURN AND TALK**

- Writers, talk about a celebration you can offer the author. What can you say about the meaning of the selection? Give compliments about the writing.

- Think together. Which words are big words? Which ones are small words? How can you tell?

If students have suggestions for changes, ask permission from the author before executing changes.

**SUM IT UP** To a class editing chart, add "Writers know that big words have more letters than small words."

**DAY 3** | **Independent Practice**

Ask writers to look in their writing folders and select a piece of writing. Give them a few minutes to reread their writing to see if their big words have more letters than the small words and if there are enough letters to match the number of sounds they hear.

 **PEER EDIT** With your writing partner, count the sounds that you hear in some of the words. Did the words have enough letters? Can you add some letters to any words? Decide together which are big words and which are small words.

 **SUM IT UP** Remember, writers, it is important to check on the length of your words. Big words have more letters than small words.

 ## Assess the Learning

- Confer with individuals to assess their ability to identify big words and small words. Record your findings on your class record-keeping grid.

- Review student writing folders and assess the samples for evidence of understanding how to stretch words and identify sounds.

 ## Link the Learning

- During writer's workshop, remind students that writers think about big words and small words so they have an idea of how many letters to write.

- In the context of small-group strategy instruction, have students frame larger and smaller words with their hands.

- Provide an opportunity for writers to review their writing folders to search for big words they have included.

- Have students examine big books and familiar stories to identify big words that have more letters, and small words that have just a few.

- Play with oral language, partnering big words with little words and thinking about the sounds in each word.

# Use Known Words to Spell Other Words

**DAY 1** | **Model the Focus Point**

Did you know that writers use words they can *already* spell, to spell other words? Here is an example: I can use the word *in*, *i-n*, to spell words like *win*, *spin*, or *win/ter*. I can use the word *at*, *a-t*, to spell *sat*, *chat*, or even a bigger word like *chatter*. Today, I am making a list of things I can write about during writer's workshop. I can write about swimming. I can spell *him*. So, if I use the *im* from *him* and add *sw*, I can write *swim*. I can write about *sand* at the beach. As I think about a word I know that will help me spell *sand*, I remember I can spell *and*! Now, all I have to do is add *s* at the beginning, and I have *sand*. This is fun!

> **Modeled Writing Sample**
>
> Ideas
>
> swim
>
> sand
>
> bike
>
> piggy bank

 **TURN AND TALK** Writers, talk to your partners when you are writing. Why is it helpful to think about words you already know how to spell?

 **SUM IT UP** Writers use words they already know, to help them spell other words when they are writing.

**DAY 2** | **Guided Practice**

Select a writing sample from a student in your class or use appendix page 185. If the author is one of your students, invite the author to read the selection to the class.

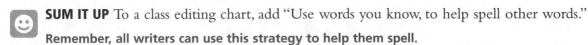

Have you ever ben on a
piknik. did ants kral in
yur fud? Did it rane.
I hope not?
            Ryan

 **TURN AND TALK**

- Writers, talk about a celebration you can offer the author. What can you say about the meaning of the selection? Give compliments about the writing.

- What did you notice about the author's spelling? Do you see places where you could use words you know, to help spell words in this writing? Are there any words in this writing that help you think of other words you might try to spell?

 **SUM IT UP** To a class editing chart, add "Use words you know, to help spell other words." Remember, all writers can use this strategy to help them spell.

Ask writers to look in their writing folders and select a piece of writing. Give them a few minutes to reread their writing. Have them find places where they could have used known words to help them spell.

 **PEER EDIT** Partners, share places where you wrote words using words you already know how to spell. Share your thinking.

 **SUM IT UP** Writers use known words to spell other words.

 ## Assess the Learning

- Observe and interview editors as they work. Use a class record-keeping grid to check off those students who are using known words to spell other words.

- Assess students as they work with rimes such as those in Tools page 161 (High-Frequency Writing Patterns/Rimes).

## Link the Learning

- During writer's workshop, remind students to use the words they already know how to spell, as they craft spellings for other words.

- Gather small groups at a pocket chart and work with sentence strips to turn rimes into a variety of words.

- Model a variety of writing pieces in which you emphasize using known words to spell other words.

- Show children how they can use a portable word wall (see Spelling Reference: Portable Word Wall, page 160, in Tools) to access known words while trying to spell a new word.

- Engage children in using tiles or sentence strips to create word families or manipulate onsets and rimes into a wide variety of familiar words.

- Show children how, during editing, they can use familiar books to look up words they want to spell.

- Model how to think together with a partner about spelling and to use known words to help each other spell additional words.

# Noticing Syllables: Each Syllable Needs a Vowel

### DAY 1    Model the Focus Point

**Today, we're learning about syllables. I'll share two rules about syllables that will help us spell. (1) We can clap words out to hear their parts. Breaking the words apart and hearing their syllables helps us spell them. Let's clap** *pencil.* (two claps) **Now let's clap** *helicopter.* (four claps) **(2) Every syllable has at least one vowel.** (Display a card with the vowels.) **When we spell a word, we check to be sure that each syllable has a vowel. I am going to write** *Fall is a beautiful time of the year.* **Help me clap** *fall.* **One clap, so it needs one vowel. If I am not sure what vowel to choose, I can put a line in the word where I know a vowel should go. When I finish writing my ideas, the lines will remind me to come back and think some more about these syllables and vowels.**

> **Modeled Writing Sample**
>
> F_l is a butf_ll time of the yer. I love all the culrs and the pils of cr_chy leevs.

 **TURN AND TALK Writers, talk to your partner about the things I did to help myself spell certain words. What did you see me doing? What did you hear me doing? What kind of letter does every syllable contain?**

😊 **SUM IT UP Writers break words apart into syllables to help spell the parts. Then they always check that each syllable has a vowel letter.**

### DAY 2    Guided Practice

Place a transparency of student writing on the overhead projector or use appendix page 176. If the author is one of your students, invite the author to read the selection to the class.

Note: Post a visual of the vowels to support partner thinking.

**TURN AND TALK**

- **Writers, talk about a celebration you can offer the author. What can you say about the meaning of the selection? Give compliments about the writing.**

- **Can you find words where the writer included a vowel in every syllable? Are there words that are missing a vowel from certain syllables?**

😊 **SUM IT UP** To a class editing chart, add "Break words into syllables to help spell the parts. Then check that each syllable has a vowel letter."

**Remember, all writers use these editing strategies.**

**DAY 3** **Independent Practice**

Ask writers to look in their writing folders and select a piece of writing. Give them a few minutes to reread their writing, checking for that important vowel letter in each syllable. Have them include a vowel or draw a line in syllables where they think a vowel has been omitted. Remind them to clap out words to identify each syllable.

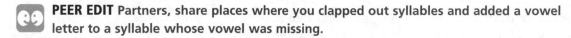 **PEER EDIT** Partners, share places where you clapped out syllables and added a vowel letter to a syllable whose vowel was missing.

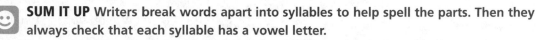 **SUM IT UP** Writers break words apart into syllables to help spell the parts. Then they always check that each syllable has a vowel letter.

## ✓ Assess the Learning

- Observe editors at work. Use a class record-keeping grid to check off those students who break words into syllables and check that each syllable has a vowel.

- Record a familiar poem or book on a chart, omitting vowels in some syllables. Pull small groups and have students identify syllables with missing vowels. Record your observations.

## ∞ Link the Learning

- During writer's workshop, remind students to use both syllable rules to help them spell.

- Gather groups of students who need additional instruction in syllables and vowels.

- Play with words orally, clapping out syllables.

- Clap out interesting words in a big book.

- Use sticky notes to mask some vowels in a big book. Encourage partners to think about which vowel may be hidden, before you uncover it.

- Encourage writers to clap out their own words during writing to help them hear the parts.

# Spelling Reference: Picture Alphabet card

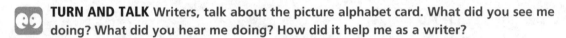

## DAY 1   Model the Focus Point

Note: Prepare a copy of the picture alphabet card from Tools page 158.

> As I write today, I will be using an alphabet card with pictures to help me find the letters and the sounds I need. I want to say, *I love summer when it's hot.* I know how to write *I*, so I can put that down. Now I am ready for *love. l-l-l* I am looking at my card, and I see a picture of a leaf. *leaf... love,* they start the same, so I can write *l.* This picture alphabet card helped a lot. Watch how I use both the letters and the pictures to help me find the letters or sounds that I want to write. If I need to, I can touch each letter as I say the alphabet to help find a certain letter or a certain sound. (Continue writing and thinking aloud to complete the piece.) **I am finished writing, so it is time to reread to see if my writing sounds the way I want it to sound. As I reread, I am going to see if I think of any more sounds that I can add.**

> **Modeled Writing Sample**
>
> Swimming
>
> By Mrs. T
>
> I lv smr. We go swming wn itz ht.
>
> (I love summer. We go swimming when it's hot.)

 **TURN AND TALK** Writers, talk about the picture alphabet card. What did you see me doing? What did you hear me doing? How did it help me as a writer?

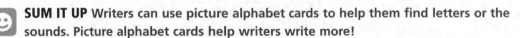 **SUM IT UP** Writers can use picture alphabet cards to help them find letters or the sounds. Picture alphabet cards help writers write more!

## DAY 2   Guided Practice

Place a student writing sample on the overhead projector, using either an example from your class or appendix page 177. If the author is one of your students, invite the author to read the selection to the class.

 **TURN AND TALK**

- Writers, talk about a celebration you can offer the author. What can you say about the meaning of the selection? Give compliments about the writing.

- Think together and use your picture alphabet cards to see if you can suggest additional letters this author might include in the writing.

If students have suggestions for changes, ask permission from the author before executing changes.

 **SUM IT UP** To a class editing chart, add "Use an alphabet card with pictures."

Remember, writers, this is an editing strategy that writers use when they are first learning their letters and sounds.

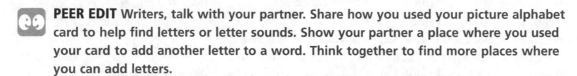 **DAY 3**  **Independent Practice**

Model reviewing papers in a writing folder, holding the picture alphabet card in your hand. Show enthusiasm when you see a place where you can use the card and think of additional letters to add to the writing. Ask your writers to look in their writing folders and select a piece of writing, and then give them a few minutes to reread and select places where they can use their cards to add more letters.

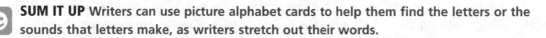 **PEER EDIT** Writers, talk with your partner. Share how you used your picture alphabet card to help find letters or letter sounds. Show your partner a place where you used your card to add another letter to a word. Think together to find more places where you can add letters.

**SUM IT UP** Writers can use picture alphabet cards to help them find the letters or the sounds that letters make, as writers stretch out their words.

## ✓ Assess the Learning

- Circulate and work with individuals to assess their ability to locate sounds and use the picture alphabet card as a tool. Use your class record-keeping grid to note those students who need additional instruction in using the card effectively, as well as those who have a solid base of letter-sound knowledge and do not need the card at all.

- Observe students as they write. Record the degree to which they independently use their picture alphabet card.

## 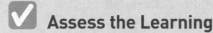 Link the Learning

- Provide modeled writing of retells, poems, summaries of daily events, and so on, using the picture alphabet card as a writing support.

- Keep the picture alphabet card in hand when conferring with individuals during writer's workshop.

- Gather a guided writing group for additional instruction in using the picture alphabet card.

- Show children how to use an picture alphabet card as a support during reading.

# Spelling Reference: Class Word Wall

## DAY 1   Model the Focus Point

Note: In advance, prepare writing that needs editing for spelling.

> **Modeled Writing Sample**
>
> Makeng chcolt chp cokees iz fn. I lik to dnk thm in mlk.

**When writers are rereading their work to check for spelling, this is a good time to use the word wall. Watch how I use the class word wall to check words. As I reread my writing, I am thinking about words that I am likely to find on the word wall. I think I am likely to see** *make* **and** *is*. **I don't think** *chocolate* **is likely to be there because it isn't a word we write every day. Watch me go to the word wall with my writing and check for** *make* **and** *is*. **They are here! I can use the wall to help me edit this writing. I will need to find another way to check on** *chocolate*.

**TURN AND TALK Talk to each other, writers, about what I did to help myself spell. When did I use the word wall?** (when I knew the word was there) **When did I stop using the word wall?** (when I couldn't quickly find a word) **When did I decide to "stretch out words" and not use the word wall?** (when I knew the word wasn't there)

**SUM IT UP Remember, writers can use a class word wall to help them quickly spell some words.**

## DAY 2   Guided Practice

Place a transparency of student writing on the overhead projector or use appendix page 182. If the author is one of your students, invite the author to read the selection to the class.

cynthia

My pet is a cine of Dog That is a (Pudole ) it's coke is white and Brown. it sound K like ruf ruffruf. I fee Love ABowt my Pudele . I Love my Pudole. she Likes chrets and erry Day. I give her a

**TURN AND TALK**

- **Writers, talk about a celebration you can offer the author. What can you say about the meaning of the selection? Give compliments about the writing.**

- **Can our word wall help the writer spell any words? Which words are most likely to be there? Which words should the writer check in another way?**

If students have suggestions for changes, ask permission from the author before executing changes.

**SUM IT UP** To a class editing chart, add "Use a class word wall to help you quickly spell some words."

**Remember, writers use a class word wall to help them spell.**

**DAY 3** **Independent Practice**

Ask writers to look in their writing folders and select a piece of writing. Give them a few minutes to reread their writing. Encourage them to find words that may be misspelled. Have them decide if the class word wall will help them or if they need to use their "stretch it out" spelling.

 **PEER EDIT** Writers, share where you used the class word wall to help you spell some words. Point out words that you "stretched out."

 **SUM IT UP** Remember, writers use a class word wall to quickly spell some words.

 **Assess the Learning**

- Use a class record-keeping grid as you observe editors at work. Determine which students are using the class word wall to find some high-frequency words, and which students need additional instruction.

- Interview individual students. Ask them to explain when and why they would and would not use a class word wall.

**Link the Learning**

- During writer's workshop, remind students that when they are editing, the word wall can help them find words that are used often in daily writing.

- For students who show evidence of understanding the word wall and high-frequency words, teach them that if they are very sure that a word is on the wall, they can occasionally use the wall during drafting. They don't want to interrupt their ideas, so they need to be very sure the word is on the wall before using it during drafting.

- Help children think about other resources they can use when they are editing for spelling. Demonstrate how to use familiar big books to find known words, look in previously created pieces of writing, confer with a friend whose name starts with the same letter, and so on.

# Spelling Reference: Portable Word Wall

## DAY 1   Model the Focus Point

Note: Prepare a portable word wall similar to the one on Tools page 160, with words that you can reasonably expect your students to spell correctly.

> When I write, I can use my own word wall to quickly spell *some* words. My Portable Word Wall can help me with the words that we see most often in writing. These are mostly little words that people expect first graders/kindergartners to spell. I'll still use my "stretch it out" spelling for all the other words. I want to write *I love to pet my cat*. I am going to check my Portable Word Wall for *love* and *my*. Those are words we use a lot, so I think they might be there. Look! There they are. This is really helpful.

**Modeled Writing Sample**

I love to pet my cat. Her fur is soft, and she purrs when I hold her.

 **TURN AND TALK** Writers, talk about the things I did to help myself spell certain words. What did you see me doing? What did you hear me doing? Did I stop to ask someone how to spell?

 **SUM IT UP** Writers use portable word walls to help them spell some words, while still using their "stretch it out" spelling for other words.

## DAY 2   Guided Practice

Place a transparency of student writing on the overhead projector or use appendix page 181 . If the author is one of your students, invite the author to read the selection to the class. Make sure to provide students with copies of portable word walls.

 **TURN AND TALK**

- Writers, talk about a celebration you can offer the author. What can you say about the meaning of the selection? Give compliments about the writing.

- Can you find words to check on the Portable Word Wall? Can you find any "stretch it out" words that won't be on the list?

 **SUM IT UP** To a class editing chart, add "Use a portable word wall to spell some words."

**DAY 3** | **Independent Practice**

Ask writers to look in their writing folders and select a piece of writing. Give students a few minutes to reread their writing, using their portable word walls and "stretch it out" spelling to edit their papers.

 **PEER EDIT** Partners, share places where you used your Portable Word Wall and then where you used the "stretch it out" strategy to help you spell.

 **SUM IT UP** Writers use portable word walls to help them spell some words, while still using their "stretch it out" spelling for other words.

## ✔ Assess the Learning

- Observe editors at work. Use a class record-keeping grid to check off those students who are using portable word walls to spell grade-level words, while still using the "stretch it out" strategy.

- Ask individuals to give a few examples of words that would most likely appear on a portable word wall, and then give examples of words that would not appear on their portable word wall. Have them explain their reasoning.

## Link the Learning

- During writer's workshop, remind students to use both their portable word walls and their "stretch it out" strategy to aid spelling.

- Refer to the High-Frequency Writing Words list in Tools, page 157, to determine appropriate words to place on portable word walls for your students. Depending on student need, some lists will have additional words; other lists will need to be shorter. Keep it manageable.

- Provide additional modeled writings in which you think aloud about words that are likely to be on a portable word wall, about when to use the resource, and about trusting yourself to stretch words out during drafting, knowing you will return to the writing as an editor.

- Encourage students to use their portable word walls as they write during math, science, social studies, and so on.

# Cycles for Improving Grammar Awareness

Reading aloud and having rich conversations with children all day long are essential building blocks of grammar development. Exposure to authors we love and the language we hear in our lives attune our ears to what "sounds right." We come to expect certain sentence structures and notice when nouns and verbs do not agree. We notice when plurals are missing or tense is misplaced. When we "float learning on a sea of talk," we maximize the potential for grammar and oral language development (J. Britton, 1970).

When focusing on grammar, take cues from your students. Listen to their oral language and look closely at the grammar embedded within their writing samples. Pay special attention to English learners and to children who come from homes where nonstandard English is spoken. With careful attention to the language patterns that are already in place, you can direct students' attention to the structures and forms woven into our read–alouds or extend and elaborate on what children say. For example, if a child says, "I goed to the store last night," your response might be, "You went to the store! How lucky for you." This elaboration and expansion of language supports and stretches learners.

# Pronoun Order: Write Person's Name and Then *I*, Not *Me*

## DAY 1 | Model the Focus Point

When I write about someone else and I'm in the story, too, I need to be polite and use the other person's name first. So, if I were writing about walking down the hall with Amanda, I would say, *Amanda and I walked down the hall*. I would not say, *Amanda and me*. I also wouldn't say, *Me and Amanda*. Today I am writing about going to a movie with my aunt. To be polite, I need to use her name first. I will write, *Aunt Sally and I love to go to funny movies*. Did you notice I remembered to say *I* rather than *me*?

> **Modeled Writing Sample**
>
> My Aunt Sally and I love to go to funny movies. We munch on popcorn, slurp from sodas, and have a great time laughing together. Aunt Sally and I could watch movies all day long!

**TURN AND TALK** Writers, think about my writing and decide, was I polite? Did I write the other person's name first? I had to decide between using *I* and *me*. How did I do?

**SUM IT UP** Remember, when you write about someone else and you're in the story, too, you need to be polite. Write the other person's name first, and then write *I* instead of the word *me*.

## DAY 2 | Guided Practice

On the overhead projector, place a transparency of student writing or use this example on appendix page 179. If the author is one of your students, invite the author to read the selection to the class.

> Marie and I both like cookies with little pieces of candy in them. One day, my mom helped Marie and me make a big batch.

**TURN AND TALK**

- Writers, talk about a celebration you can offer the author. What can you say about the meaning of the selection? Give compliments about the writing.

- Decide with your partner: Was the author polite? Why or why not? Did the author put the other person's name first, and then use *I* instead of *me*?

If students have suggestions, ask permission from the author before executing the changes.

**SUM IT UP** To a class editing chart, add "Write the other person's name first, and then write *I*, instead of *me*. (Example: *José and I*)

Remember, writers do this whenever they write or talk!

**DAY 3** | **Independent Practice**

Ask writers to look in their writing folders and select a piece of writing in which they wrote about someone else but included themselves in the story, too. Give them a few minutes to reread to determine if they were polite by writing the other person's name first, and then writing *I* instead of *me*.

 **PEER EDIT** Share where you wrote about someone else, and you were in the story, too. Were you polite? Did you write the other person's name first, and then write *I* instead of *me*?

 **SUM IT UP** Remember, when you write about another person and yourself, put the other person's name first.

 ## Assess the Learning

- Use a class record-keeping grid as you observe editors at work. Check off those students who are writing the other person's name first, and then writing *I* instead of *me*.

- Ask individual students to relate an experience they shared with someone else. Record their use of the other person's name first, and then their use of *I* instead of *me*.

## Link the Learning

- During writer's workshop, remind students that when they write about someone else and include themselves in the story, too, they should write the other person's name first, and then write *I* instead of *me*. Help writers apply what they know as they craft writing selections.

- Have student meet with partners and take turns creating sentences that follow the grammatical pattern, for example, *Siella and I played on the swings* and *Armando and I played wall ball*.

- During read-alouds or shared reading point out when the author writes the other person's name, and then writes *I*, not *me*. (Examples: *A Chair for My Mother* by Vera Williams or *The Wednesday Surprise* by Eve Bunting)

- Encourage children to describe family activities with stems such as *My mother and I* and *My brother and I*.

# Complete Sentences

## DAY 1   Model the Focus Point

Note: Create a chart with these two questions: *Who or what did something? What did they do?*

> **To create a complete sentence, we need to tell "who or what did something" and then tell "what they did." I wrote, *My dog runs really fast*. Let's check it against those two important questions on our chart and see how I did. Did I tell who or what did something? Yes. I said, *my dog*. Did I tell what my dog did? Yes. *My dog runs really fast*. I made a complete sentence! Let's try another one. Remember, sentences need to tell "who or what did something" and "what they did."**

 **TURN AND TALK** Writers, tell each other which sentence you enjoyed. Look at our chart and talk about my sentences. How did I do at answering the key questions for a complete sentence?

 **SUM IT UP** Remember, a complete sentence has two parts: the part that tells "who or what did something" and the part that tells "what they did." Writers have a sentence with both parts.

---

### Modeled Writing Sample

My dog runs really fast. He races around the kitchen and slides under the chairs.

---

## DAY 2   Guided Practice

Display a piece of student writing or use appendix page 173. If the author is one of your students, invite the author to read the selection to the class.

The moon sion on the Earth

 **TURN AND TALK**

- Talk about a celebration you can offer the author. What can you say about the meaning of the selection?

- Now, think together about writing complete sentences. Look at our chart with the two important questions about sentences. Did the author include "who or what did something" and "what they did"?

If students have suggestions, ask permission from the author before executing the changes.

 **SUM IT UP** To a class editing chart, add "Sentences have two main parts: the 'who or what did something' and 'what they did.' (Examples: Kids run. My best friend runs fast!)

**DAY 3** | **Independent Practice**

Ask writers to look in their writing folders and select a piece of writing. Give them a few minutes to reread to determine which sentences they liked the best and if their sentences had both parts.

 **PEER EDIT** Writers, show your partners your favorite sentences. Then show the two parts of your sentences. Did you find a place where you had left out a part of the sentence? Did you go back and add the missing part?

 **SUM IT UP** Remember, a complete sentence has two parts: the part that tells "who or what did something" and the part that tells "what they did." Writers can't have a sentence without both parts.

 **Assess the Learning**

- Review writing folders to determine which students are writing complete sentences. Use a class record-keeping grid (see Assessment and Record Keeping page 170) to record your findings.

- Have students select a piece of writing. Then have them identify the "who or what did something" and the "what they did." Record their understandings.

**Link the Learning**

- During writer's workshop, remind students to use the chart created at the beginning of this cycle with the two special questions as they check their work for complete sentences.

- During shared reading, examine selected sentences to see if the two key questions about complete sentences are answered.

- Provide typed copies of a portion of a shared reading text and have students circle in pencil the "who or what did something" in a sentence; then have them underline the "what they did."

- During small-group instruction, have students find sentences in their books that answer the two key questions on the chart.

- Teach children to examine their own illustrations using the questions from the chart created at the beginning of this cycle. Do the illustrations show "who or what did something" and "what they did"?

# Single vs. Double Subject
# (My mom vs. My mom, she)

### DAY 1    Model the Focus Point

**I want to write about my friend Mary. We have been friends for many years, and I know we will be friends forever.** (Begin writing, *Mary, she,* and then stop and self-correct by crossing through the word *she*.) **Did you see what I just did? I wrote *Mary* and then I wrote *she*. I only need to tell you once who I am talking about. I will write, *Mary is my best friend*. That is better. In my second sentence, I want to say that she is funny. I need to decide if I should say, *Mary, she makes me laugh* or *She makes me laugh*. I don't want to double up again, so I will say *She makes me laugh*. I have to remember that I only need to tell whom I am talking about one time in each sentence.**

> **Modeled Writing Sample**
>
> Mary is my best friend. She makes me laugh I know we will be friends forever!

**TURN AND TALK** Writers, what was I careful NOT to do? What do we need to remember?

**SUM IT UP** Remember, writers only need to tell whom they are talking about *one time* in each sentence. When writing about someone and using his or her name, don't write *he* or *she* in the same sentence. That is too much.

### DAY 2    Guided Practice

Use this example from appendix page 179 or display a student writing sample on the overhead. If the author is one of your students, invite the author to read the selection to the class.

> Brownie he likes to play catch. Brownie he jumps and runs and brings balls and sticks right back to me. I love him.

 **TURN AND TALK**

- **Writers, talk about a celebration you can offer the author. What can you say about the meaning of the selection? Give compliments about the writing.**

- **Think together. We have been trying to remember to tell whom we are talking about only *one time* in each sentence. What suggestions do we have for this writing?**

If students have suggestions, ask permission from the author before executing the changes.

**SUM IT UP** To a class editing chart, add "Write *My mom*. <u>Don't</u> write *My mom, she*… **Remember, writers write only the person's name or *he* or *she*. Don't write both in the same sentence.**

**DAY 3** | **Independent Practice**

Ask writers to look in their writing folders and select a piece of writing in which they wrote about someone else. Give them a few minutes to reread to determine if they followed the rule: *(Post the rule/example.)* Write "My mom." Don't write "My mom, she."

**PEER EDIT** Share a place where you wrote about someone else. Show your partner a place where you remembered to tell only once whom you were talking about. Show your partner a place where you realized you had told whom you were talking about more than once in the same sentence.

**SUM IT UP** Writers need to remember that you can tell who you are talking about only one time in each sentence.

## ✔ Assess the Learning

- Closely examine writing samples and oral language patterns to determine which students are still using double subjects in either oral or written language.

- Listen in on children's conversations to determine which students are still using double subjects in oral language. Record your findings on a grid labeled "Grammar," with a column identified as "Uses Double Subjects."

## ∞ Link the Learning

- Gather students who are still using double subjects into small groups for oral language experiences. Help them by providing language stems such as these: *My mother* _____. *My father* _____. *My friend* _____.

- During writer's workshop, remind students that when writing about someone/something, they can tell whom they are talking about only one time in each sentence. (This applies to simple sentences only.)

- FYI: Compound subjects such as "My mom and dad" are correct. Double subjects like "My mom, she" are incorrect because they name the same person two times.

- During read-alouds or shared reading, highlight sentences and have children think together about double subjects. Did the author tell *who* more than once?

- Use a pocket chart to display sentences with double subjects, such as *My mother, she* _____. Using scissors, work with the students to remove the double subjects from the sentences.

# Using Transition Words

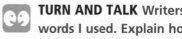 **DAY 1**  **Model the Focus Point**

Transition words are words that connect ideas, alert the reader that something is coming, or show sequence. Some transition words you see a lot are *first*, *next*, *now*, *then*, and *finally*. As I write about making soup, notice how I use transition words to show the order in which things happen and to alert the reader to pay attention to what is coming. It is important to know that a comma usually follows a transition word. Commas and transition words are great buddies!

 **TURN AND TALK** Writers, tell each other what transition words I used. Explain how transitions help a reader. What punctuation mark is usually seen with a transition word?

 **SUM IT UP** Remember, use transition words to alert the reader of things to come, suggest order, or link ideas together. A transition word is usually followed by a comma.

> **Modeled Writing Sample**
>
> Making Soup
>
> <u>First</u>, open the can and pour the soup into a pan. <u>Next</u>, pour in a can of water. <u>Now</u>, it's time to turn on the stove. <u>Then</u>, you wait until it gets hot. <u>Finally</u>, it's time to eat the soup.

**DAY 2**  **Guided Practice**

Note: It will help if you have transition words already written on sentence strips. Display appendix page 180 in a pocket chart and explain that everyone is going to work together to insert transition words.

 **TURN AND TALK**
- Writers, talk about a celebration you can offer the author. What can you say about the meaning of the selection? Give compliments about the writing.
- Think together about using transition words to show sequence and important ideas that are coming. Where could transition words be added? Where should the comma go?

**SUM IT UP** To a class editing chart, add "Use transition words and their buddy, the comma." Remember, writers use transition words to let readers know of things to come.

> *Making a Peanut Butter and Jelly Sandwich*
>
> You need to get the peanut butter, jelly, two pieces of bread, and knife out. Spread the peanut butter on one piece of bread. Spread the jelly on top of the peanut butter. Put the other piece of bread on top of all of that. Cut the sandwich into pieces. Eat!

Post transition words and ask writers to look in their folders for a piece of writing in which they used transition words or could add transition words.

 **PEER EDIT** Share places where you have used transition words and their buddy, the comma.

 **SUM IT UP** Remember, use transition words to alert the reader of things to come, connect ideas, or suggest sequence. A transition word is usually followed by a comma.

##  Assess the Learning

- Use a class record-keeping grid as you observe editors at work. Identify those students who use transition words followed by a comma in multiple writing samples. Gather other students into small groups for continued support and instruction.

- Ask individual students to explain how to do something, such as make a peanut butter and jelly sandwich. Check for use of transition words. Document your observations.

##  Link the Learning

- Post lists of transition words where writers can see them easily. You might consider posting words such as these: *before, after, now, first, then, finally, next, but, soon, once, now, right before, whenever, one day, so, suddenly, because, when, just.*

- During writer's workshop, remind students to use transition words to support their ideas.

- At the end of shared reading, count the transition words used in the selection. Use highlighter tape to highlight places where a comma followed the transition word.

- During small-group instruction, provide sticky notes and encourage students to add some transition words to the guided reading selections.

# Singular and Plural Nouns

**DAY 1**  **Model the Focus Point**

Who likes cookies? I do! I could eat just one cookie, but I always find myself wishing for lots of cookies. I am going to write *cookie* and *cookies* on my paper. Do you see the *s* at the end of *cookies*? Adding an *s* is one of the ways in which we can show that there is more than one. Let's try some more: Here is one pencil. Now I am holding lots of pencils. Watch me write *pencil*. Now, what letter should I add? When there is only one of something, we say it is singular. It is a "single" one. When there is more than one, that is called a "plural."

| Modeled Writing Sample | |
| --- | --- |
| Singular | Plural |
| cookie | cookies |
| pencil | pencils |
| book | books |
| crayon | crayons |

 **TURN AND TALK** Writers, talk to your partners. What did you notice about the way I wrote my singular and plural words? Think together. Can you think of a thing that you can name and then add an *s*?

**SUM IT UP** Writers pay attention to whether something is singular or plural when they are writing.

**DAY 2**  **Guided Practice**

Select a writing sample from a student in your class or use the one from appendix page 189. If the author is one of your students, invite the author to read the selection to the class.

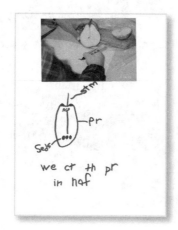

 **TURN AND TALK**

• Writers, talk about a celebration you can offer the author. What can you say about the meaning of the selection? Give compliments about the writing.

• Think about singular and plural. How many pears are there? Should the word *pear* have an *s* at the end?

**SUM IT UP** To a class editing chart, add "Add *s* when there is more than one."

Writers can use this spelling strategy to help them spell.

**DAY 3** **Independent Practice**

Ask writers to look in their writing folders and select a piece of writing. Give them a few minutes to reread their writing. Have them find places where they could add an *s* to show there is more than one.

 **PEER EDIT** Partners, share places in your writing that show just one item. Show each other a place where you added *s* if there was more than one.

 **SUM IT UP** Spellers, remember to add an *s* to the end of some words to show that there is more than one item.

 **Assess the Learning**

- Observe and interview editors as they work. Use a class record-keeping grid to check off those students who are able to differentiate between singular and plural, with the addition of *s*.

- Ask writers to create a T-chart. Have them list singular things they can write about in one column, and plural things in the other column. Assess for singular and plural understandings. Then have writers save their idea lists in their writing folders.

**Link the Learning**

- Look for examples of singular and plural in familiar big books.

- Fill a pocket chart with pictures and words that could be transformed from singular to plural by adding *s*. Invite the children to work with the words and make them into plurals.

- Model a variety of writing pieces in which you think out loud about whether you should make a word singular or plural.

- Engage children in using tiles or sentence strips to add *s* to some words to make them plural.

# Singular Subject-Verb Agreement

**DAY 1** | **Model the Focus Point**

It is important to notice that when we are writing about something happening right now, in the present, the action word (verb) needs to match the subject. Watch. Here is my first sentence, *Mrs. T runs*. Mrs. T is just one person, so we have an *s* on *runs*. Here is a different one, *The students run*. This isn't one person anymore; it is lots of people. Notice that the *s* isn't on *run* anymore. Let's do some more. The girl *skips*. Notice the *s* on the action word *skips*. The girls *skip*. We now have lots of girls, so there is not an *s*. . . just the word *skip*. We make this little change when we talk. Now, we need to think about these things when we write!

> **Modeled Writing Sample**
>
> Mrs. T run<u>s</u>.     The students run.
>
> The girl skip<u>s</u>.     The girls skip.
>
> Julio hop<u>s</u>.       The boys hop.
>
> The child sit<u>s</u>.     The children sit.

 **TURN AND TALK** Writers, what did you notice about my writing today. What happened when I wrote about a single person? What changed when I wrote about lots of people?

 **SUM IT UP** When writers write about *one* person, place, or thing, action words are likely to end in *s*.

**DAY 2** | **Guided Practice**

Display a sample of a singular subject and an action verb with *s* from a student example or use appendix page 181. If the author is one of your students, invite the author to read the selection to the class.

 **TURN AND TALK**

- Writers, talk about a celebration you can offer the author. What can you say about the meaning of the selection? Give compliments about the writing.

- Is the writing about a single person or thing? If so, can you find any action verbs with an *s* at the end? What else do you notice?

If students have suggestions for changes, ask permission from the author before executing the changes.

 **SUM IT UP** To a class editing chart, add "When writing about one person, place, or thing, use action words that end in *s*."

**Remember, writers do this when writing.**

Have writers look in their folders and select a piece of writing in which they wrote about just one person, place, or thing. Give them a few minutes to check their work to see if they have any action words ending in *s*.

 **PEER EDIT** Share places in your writing where you wrote about just one person, place, or thing. Think together about whether you had any action verbs ending in *s* or have an idea about where to add an *s*.

 **SUM IT UP** When writers write about *one* person, place, or thing, action verbs often end in *s*.

 ## Assess the Learning

- Use the spaces at the top of a class record-keeping grid to list oral use of singular, plural, and singular subject-verb agreement, as well as written use of these forms. Tally those students who control these forms orally, as well as those who use these forms correctly in their writing.

- During silent reading, ask students about the subject and verb in their selection. Have them determine if the book is talking about a singular subject. Ask for their reasoning.

## Link the Learning

- Gather in a small group those students who need oral support, and practice grouping real items into singles and groups with many things. With each real item, engage children with language stems such as these: *This pencil is red. These pencils are red.*

- During writer's workshop, remind students that if they are writing about a single person, place, or thing, they may want to use action verbs ending in *s*.

- Review familiar big books for singular subject-verb agreement. Pull out favorite sentences with singular subject-verb agreement and place them in a pocket chart. Work with children to turn the subject into a plural and then make the verb agree.

- When you have "wait" time in line, use it to play with language, making subject/verb agreement fun and lively. To help children understand that subject/verb agreement doesn't require the use of a personal name, try stems such as these: *He runs. They run. She skips. They skip.*

# Plural Subject-Verb Agreement

## DAY 1    Model the Focus Point

Create a T-chart. Label it *singular* and *plural*.

**We have been learning about singular and plural. Today, we are going to talk about what happens to verbs when we write about lots of things or lots of people. For example, if I say, *He runs*, that is a single person, and the action verb gets an *s*. If I say, *They run*, look what happens. This is about lots of people, and there is no *s* on the action verb. I will write that on my chart. We have practiced this before. Let's make it trickier! I will write *She is swimming*. Then I will change it to *They are swimming*. What happened? Look closely. What do you notice?**

| Modeled Writing Sample | |
|---|---|
| Singular Subject | Plural Subject |
| He runs. | They run. |
| She is swimming. | They are swimming. |
| The teacher is writing. | They are writing. |
| The worm is crawling. | The worms are crawling. |

 **TURN AND TALK** Writers, what have you noticed about the words in my writing?

 **SUM IT UP** When writing about *two or more* people, places, or things, pay attention to the verb. It is not the same as when writing about one person or one thing.

## DAY 2    Guided Practice

Display appendix page 176 or a writing sample from one of your students. If the author is one of your students, invite the author to read the selection to the class.

 **TURN AND TALK**

- **Writers, talk about a celebration you can offer the author. What can you say about the meaning of the selection? Give compliments about the writing.**

- **Look at each sentence. Think together. Is this sentence about one person or many people? What do you notice about the verbs?**

If students have suggestions for changes, ask permission from the author before executing the changes.

 **SUM IT UP** To a class editing chart, add "When writing about two or more people, places, or things, pay attention to the verbs."

**DAY 3** | **Independent Practice**

Ask writers to look in their folders and select a piece of writing in which they wrote about two or more people, places, or things. Give them a few minutes to check their papers for plural subjects and agreeing verbs.

 **PEER EDIT** Share your thinking with your editing partner. Show each other places where you wrote about more than one person, place, or thing. Look at your verbs together. What do you notice?

 **SUM IT UP** When writing about *two or more* people, places, or things, writers pay attention to the verbs.

 **Assess the Learning**

- Using the Class Record-Keeping Grid prepared in the lesson on singular subject-verb agreement, continue to assess understanding of singular and plural agreement in both oral and written language samples.

- Give students "flags" made from sticky notes. First, have them flag plural subjects and their verbs in familiar books or their own writing. Record their understandings. Then, have them do the same for singular nouns and their verbs.

**Link the Learning**

- Engage in several modeled writings in which you think aloud about singular and plural and then ask children for advice about which verbs you should select.

- During writer's workshop, remind students to use plural subject-verb agreements.

- Select sentences with plural subject-verb agreement from familiar read-alouds. Place the sentences in a pocket chart. Read them with students and then convert each plural sentence into a singular sentence by changing the subject and the verb.

- Create a bulletin board of terrific plural sentences and spectacular singular sentences from favorite books. Write the sentences on sentence strips and post them next to photocopies of the covers of the books from which they were selected.

- Have small groups of children work together to cluster singular and plural sentences.

- During small-group reading, have children determine if sentences are about singular or plural subjects, and then look at the verbs.

# Past-Tense Verbs

## DAY 1 | Model the Focus Point

When we write about things that have already happened, we need to choose verbs carefully. Verbs are really important in helping our readers understand our meaning. I am going to write about the first day of school. That was a while ago, wasn't it! Watch while I write, *My heart was thumping, and I felt as jumpy...* I am going to stop for a minute. If this was happening right now, this writing would sound different. I wrote, *my heart was thumping.* That tells a reader that it already happened. If this was happening right now, I would have said, *My heart is thumping!* I need to be really careful with the words I select. I want to tell how I looked at the clock. I am thinking, *Should I say look or looked?* Which is better to tell that this has already happened? That is right. Sometimes we show past tense by adding *-ed* to our verbs.

> **Modeled Writing Sample**
>
> My heart was thumping and I felt as jumpy as can be. I looked at the clock and noticed that my new students would be arriving any minute.

 **TURN AND TALK** Writers, talk about my verbs. What did you notice? How do my verbs change when I am telling about something in the past?

 **SUM IT UP** Remember, when something has already happened, writers need to choose verbs carefully to show that this was in the past.

## DAY 2 | Guided Practice

Display appendix page 181 on sentence strips in a pocket chart. Invite children to work with you to read the selection before beginning partner conversations. After their conversations, work with the class to revise the piece and insert conventional, past-tense verbs.

> **Saturday at the Park**
>
> It snowed on Saturday. We goed to the park. It was beautiful! I wanted to stay forever. It lookt like winter. We goded home before it got dark.

 **TURN AND TALK**

- Writers, talk about a celebration you can offer the author. What can you say about the meaning of the selection? Give compliments about the writing.

- Now, how did the author show us that this has already happened? Look closely at the verbs. I think that you will have some good ideas for this.

If students have suggestions, ask permission from the author before executing the changes.

**SUM IT UP** To a class editing chart, add "Use past-tense verbs when telling about things that have already happened."

**DAY 3** | **Independent Practice**

Ask writers to look in their writing folders and use sticky notes to identify points where they wrote about something that has already happened. Encourage them to think about their verbs. Do their verbs help show that this has already happened?

 **PEER EDIT** Show each other how you wrote about things that have already happened. Think together about the verbs.

 **SUM IT UP** Remember, when something has already happened, writers look closely at the verbs to show past tense.

## ✔ Assess the Learning

- Review writing folders and editors at work. Check off those students who use *-ed* endings on action verbs to indicate past tense, and those who use an irregular form to change the verb form.

- Ask writers to write about something that has already happened. Have them use sticky notes to "flag" the verbs. Assess their understanding of past-tense verbs.

##  Link the Learning

- During writer's workshop, remind students to decide if they are writing about right now or something in the past, and to use what they know about helping their reader by using past-tense verbs.

- Begin a three-column Verb Resource Chart. Revise the chart as your students' understanding evolves. Encourage students to look for past-tense verbs in their reading selections so you can add their discoveries to the chart.

| REGULAR VERBS | | REGULAR VERBS | | IRREGULAR | | | |
|---|---|---|---|---|---|---|---|
| (-ed ending, sounds like /d/) | | (-ed ending, sounds like /t/) | | (different word/past tense) | | | |
| count | counted | walk | walked | sit | sat | write | wrote |
| hunt | hunted | like | liked | eat | ate | sing | sang |
| open | opened | stop | stopped | is | was | are | were |

- Engage children in a scavenger hunt for past-tense verbs in familiar stories. When they find an example in which something has already happened, celebrate and compare their discovery to the Verb Resource Chart.

# Possessive Pronouns

## DAY 1 | Model the Focus Point

Prepare a sentence strip with the words *his*, *her*, *its*, and *their*.

**Writers, here are four important words that I see in your writing all the time: *his*, *her*, *its*, and *their*. These possessive pronouns show us that something belongs to someone. I am writing about my dog's toys. The nice thing about possessive pronouns is that they save me from having to say my dog's name over and over and over in my writing. Watch as I write and get ready to tell your partner every time you see me use a possessive pronoun!**

 **TURN AND TALK Writers, talk about the possessive pronouns I used. Which ones did you notice? What would this have sounded like if I hadn't used possessive pronouns and had kept saying *Oakley* over and over and over again?**

 **SUM IT UP Remember, writers use the possessive pronouns *his*, *her*, *its*, and *their* to show ownership, without having to use the person's name over and over.**

> **Modeled Writing Sample**
>
> Oakley and Her Toys
>
> My dog, Oakley, loves her toys. She likes to carry her ball, her rope, and her chewy toy, all at once! If another dog comes around, she is quick to defend her special collection. We have had other dogs, but none loved their toys as much as Oakley.

## DAY 2 | Guided Practice

Make a transparency of appendix page 178. Have the children join you in a shared reading of the selection and then engage in partner conversations. After their conversations, work with children to select possessive pronouns to insert into the writing.

 **TURN AND TALK**

- **Writers, talk about a celebration you can offer the author. What can you say about the meaning of the selection? Give compliments about the writing.**

- **Try placing some of the possessive pronouns in the blanks. Which ones will work?**

 **SUM IT UP** To a class editing chart, add "Show ownership with possessive pronouns."

> Once upon a time there was a little old woman who loved ____ books. She arranged ____ books in every room in ____ house and filled up so many spaces that her family didn't have anywhere to place ____ own special treasures.

**DAY 3** | **Independent Practice**

Ask writers to look in their writing folders and select a piece of writing in which they used possessive pronouns. Post the list of possessive pronouns. Give students a few minutes to reread and identify places where they have used them in their writing.

 **PEER EDIT** Share where you used the possessive pronouns *his, her, its,* or *their*. When did you use *her*? *his*? *its*? *their*? Why are possessive pronouns helpful to a writer?

 **SUM IT UP** Remember, writers use the possessive pronouns *his, her, its,* and *their* to show ownership.

## ✔️ Assess the Learning

- Use a class record-keeping grid as you observe editors at work. Check off those students who use possessive pronouns in their writing and in oral speech.

- Have students locate and record possessive pronouns from their favorite books. Record their understandings.

##  Link the Learning

- Those students who do not yet have this understanding can be gathered into a brief guided writing experience in which you might again model and guide them as they use possessive pronouns.

- During writer's workshop, remind students to use possessive pronouns.

- Find examples of possessive pronouns in favorite fiction selections. Have children select their favorite sentences with possessive pronouns and copy them onto sentence strips to post on a bulletin board.

- Collect writing samples in which students use too many possessive pronouns, and invite the class to think together about the writing. How do writers decide how many possessive pronouns are the right amount? What happens to the writing when they forget to identify the name of the person or object they are writing about?

# Cycles for Lifting Punctuation

**W**ell-designed punctuation controls the flow of a message, helps the reader understand nuances of meaning, and makes the texts we construct more interesting! Punctuation should not be limited to end-of-process corrections; rather, it should be recast as a tool we use to shape our thoughts. Our objective is to support writers in understanding that punctuation, when thoughtfully used, can lift the quality of our writing. With this in mind, we coach writers to think about punctuation at two significant points in the writing process:

1. **During drafting:** Here, punctuation turns our thinking toward interesting phrasing; for example, if we add onomatopoeia and interjections, which stimulate emotion in the reader, we might also want to include exclamation points.

2. **During editing:** This is where we reread for conventional use and ensure that we have applied punctuation that will help a reader navigate our work.

Above all, we focus on transferring knowledge of punctuation across a wide variety of contexts so that writers generalize their knowledge and can apply appropriate punctuation across all texts.

# Periods: End of Sentence

## DAY 1   Model the Focus Point

Please link this lesson cycle to the lesson cycle on "Complete Sentences," pages 80 and 81 of the grammar section of this resource. Display a chart that has these questions: *Who or what did something? What did they do?*

> **Writers, to create a complete sentence, we need to tell "who or what did something" and then tell "what they did." If our work can answer both of those questions, we are ready to use a period to show that the sentence is finished. I will start by writing *My husband*... Let's check to see if I can add a period yet. Did I tell *who*? Yes, I did. Did I tell *what that person did*? No... I can't use a period yet. *My husband likes to start each day by taking*... Am I ready for a period? Did I tell what he did yet? Okay. I will keep going. Help me decide when I am ready for a period at the end of sentences that tell us something.**

 **TURN AND TALK** Writers, talk with your partner about my *sentences*. How many periods did I use? How do we know when we are ready for a period?

 **SUM IT UP** Remember, writers often use a period to end sentences that tell us something.

---

### Modeled Writing Sample

**Starting the Day**

My husband likes to start each day by taking our dog for a walk. He and the dog head for their favorite path, with big smiles on their faces.

---

## DAY 2   Guided Practice

Display appendix page 186 or a writing sample from your students. If the author is one of your students, invite the author to read the selection to the class.

 **TURN AND TALK**

- Writers, talk about a celebration you can offer the author. What can you say about the meaning of the selection? Give compliments about the writing.

- Did the author put a period at the end of all the sentences? What else did the writer do to show a sentence has ended?

If students have suggestions for changes, receive permission from the author before executing the changes.

 **SUM IT UP** To a class editing chart, add "Use a period at the end of declarative sentences."

Remember, writers use a period at the end of all "telling sentences."

Ask writers to look in their writing folders and select a piece of writing in which they wrote "telling sentences," that is, declarative sentences. Give them a few minutes to find places where they either remembered to use periods or edited to add periods.

 **PEER EDIT** Now, share your favorite sentences and show how you knew where to place the periods.

 **SUM IT UP** Remember, writers always end a declarative sentence, "a telling sentence," with a period.

 ## Assess the Learning

- Use a class record-keeping grid as you observe editors at work. Check off those students who use periods to end declarative sentences.

- Have students survey big books and count sentences with periods. Have them count sentences that have other end punctuation. Record your observations.

## Link the Learning

- During writer's workshop, remind students to use periods at the end of declarative sentences.

- In guided reading, have students count the periods and use the two key questions to determine if the periods are in the right place.

- Place a familiar text on sentence strips in a pocket chart but do not include periods. Have children decide where the periods need to be placed.

- Enlarge the text of a page from a guided selection and have children cut the words apart and scramble them. Then have them decide where the periods should be placed.

# Question Marks: Interrogative Sentences

## DAY 1   Model the Focus Point

We know that we use a period at the end of a sentence that tells us something. When we write questions, we need a different kind of punctuation. We need a question mark to tell the reader or the listener that they need to respond. Let's practice. I will write the questions; then you can provide the answers after I place my question marks on the page. I'm interested in your opinions. So, watch and listen as I write some questions to ask you.

 **TURN AND TALK** Writers, talk with your partner about my questions. What did I put at the end of each question? What is the purpose of a question?

 **SUM IT UP** Remember, we always end an interrogative sentence, an "asking sentence," with a question mark.

> **Modeled Writing Sample**
>
> What is your favorite color?
>
> Who is the kindest person you know?
>
> Where is your favorite place to read a book?
>
> What do you like to do after school?

## DAY 2   Guided Practice

Display appendix page 185 or a student writing that includes questions. If the author is one of your students, invite the author to read the selection to the class.

 **TURN AND TALK**

- Writers, talk about a celebration you can offer the author. What can you say about the meaning of the selection? Give compliments about the writing.

- Now, tell each other what belongs at the end of a question. Did the author put a question mark at the end of all the sentences? How many sentences asked a question? How many question marks were needed?

> Have you ever ben on a Piknik. did ants kral in yur fud? Did it rane. I hope not?
>
> Ryan

If students have suggestions for changes, receive permission from the author before executing the changes.

 **SUM IT UP** To a class editing chart, add "Use a question mark at the end of interrogative sentences."

Remember, writers use a question mark at the end of all "questioning sentences."

Ask writers to look in their writing folders and select a piece of writing in which they asked some questions. Give them a few minutes to reread for the use of a question mark at the end of an interrogative sentence. Have them find places where they either remembered to use question marks or edited to include them.

 **PEER EDIT** Now, share the places where you ended questions with question marks. Were there places where you added a question mark to an interrogative sentence?

 **SUM IT UP** Remember, we always end an interrogative sentence, an "asking sentence," with a question mark.

## ✓ Assess the Learning

- Gather writing folders and assess to determine which students are incorporating questions into their writing.

- Record your observations from the 3"x5"-card activity suggested in Link the Learning (below).

##  Link the Learning

- During writer's workshop, remind students to use question marks at the end of interrogative sentences.

- Those students who do not yet have this understanding can be gathered into a brief guided writing experience in which you might again model and guide the use of question marks.

- Model writing questions as headings for a nonfiction piece of writing.

- Give each student a 3"x5" card with a question mark written on one side and a period on the other. Orally present a variety of sentences and questions, and have children decide which kind of end punctuation is needed for each.

- Model being "Detective Question Mark" by circling all question marks in a newspaper or copied article or by placing clear acetate over a book and marking question marks on the acetate cover.

# Exclamation Points: Exclamatory Sentences and Interjections

## DAY 1 · Model the Focus Point

Writers, did you know that sentences that show strong feeling often end with an exclamation point? As I write, notice how I put an exclamation point at the end of sentences—or even after a single word—that show a strong emotion. I am writing about my morning cereal. I just love the noise it makes when I pour in the milk. I will write *Snap! Crackle!* Notice how I use exclamation points after just the words. That tells my reader to read these with gusto!

> **Modeled Writing Sample**
>
> Noises in My Bowl
>
> Snap! Crackle! As I pour the milk on my cereal in the morning, I love to listen to the happy noises erupting from my bowl. I love it!

 **TURN AND TALK** Writers, talk with your partner about my sentences that showed a strong feeling. What kind of strong emotion was I sharing? Notice that I used exclamation points after some single words, too. Talk about that.

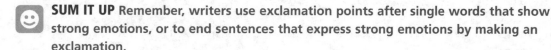 **SUM IT UP** Remember, writers use exclamation points after single words that show strong emotions, or to end sentences that express strong emotions by making an exclamation.

## DAY 2 · Guided Practice

Display appendix page 186 or a student writing sample that has or could have exclamation points added. If the author is one of your students, invite the author to read the selection to the class.

 **TURN AND TALK**

- Writers, talk about a celebration you can offer the author. What can you say about the meaning of the selection? Give compliments about the writing.

- Tell each other what belongs at the end of every exclamatory sentence or after a single word that shows strong feelings. How many sentences expressed a strong feeling? How many exclamation points were needed? Did any sentences use a period? Why?

If students have suggestions for changes, receive permission from the author before executing the changes.

**SUM IT UP** To a class editing chart, add "Use an exclamation point at the end of sentences and single words that express strong feelings."

Remember, writers use exclamation points when their writing shows a strong emotion.

MECHANICS: GRADES K–1

**DAY 3** | **Independent Practice**

Ask writers to look in their writing folders and select a piece of writing in which they expressed strong emotions. Give them a few minutes to reread for the use of exclamation points when showing strong emotions.

 **PEER EDIT** Share the places where you used exclamation points to show strong feelings. Were there places where you changed your punctuation from a period to an exclamation point? How did using an exclamation point change the meaning of your sentence?

 **SUM IT UP** Remember, writers use exclamation points at the end of exclamatory sentences and after single words that show strong emotions.

 **Assess the Learning**

- Gather small groups around a pocket chart in which you have placed several sentences that do not have end punctuation. Assess students' ability to identify punctuation for each line. They should have an opportunity to insert a period, a question mark, an exclamation point for an interjection, and an exclamation point for an exclamatory sentence.

- Have writers select two writing samples that use exclamation points, and record your observations.

**Link the Learning**

- During writer's workshop, remind students to use exclamation points to show strong emotions.

- Have partners survey big books to search for places where authors use exclamation points, or places where students could use sticky notes and add them.

- Read *Don't Let the Pigeon Drive the Bus* by Mo Willems, *Yo! Yes?* by Chris Raschka, and *Punctuation Takes a Vacation* by Robin Pulver. Have children enjoy and discuss the exclamation points along with the other punctuation used in these books.

- Have children work in pairs to create sentences that show strong feeling, and to punctuate them with exclamation points. Display their sentences on an "Exclamations!" bulletin board.

- Revisit the earlier passage on page 102:

   Noises in My Bowl

   Snap! Crackle! As I pour the milk on my cereal in the morning, I *love* to listen to the happy noises erupting from my bowl. I *love* it!

Help children understand that strong words—like *love*—also convey emotion, but we don't always have to pair every strong word with an exclamation point. Too many exclamation points can actually weaken the writing. Children will learn that exclamation points are very special and should be used sparingly.

# Commas: Use in a Series

## DAY 1 | Model the Focus Point

When writers write about one thing after another in the same sentence, they use a comma to separate each thing. The comma tells the reader to take a little pause. If I write about what I had for breakfast, I'd write *For breakfast I had an egg, bacon, toast, and a big glass of milk*. Did you notice how I used a comma between each item I ate? Notice also that for my very last item, I use the word *and* to show that this is the end of my list.

 **TURN AND TALK** Writers, think about the commas I used. Why did I use them? Where did I write the comma, on the line or floating above the line? What do commas tell the reader to do?

 **SUM IT UP** When writers write about several things in one sentence, they use commas to separate those things. Then they write the word *and* before the last item. This is called using commas in a series.

> ### Modeled Writing Sample
>
> For breakfast I had an egg, bacon, toast, and a big glass of milk. My husband was even hungrier! He had an egg, bacon, toast, a big glass of milk, and orange juice.

## DAY 2 | Guided Practice

Display appendix page 180 or a student writing sample that includes items in a series. If the author is one of your students, invite the author to read the selection to the class.

 **TURN AND TALK**

- Writers, talk about a celebration you can offer the author. What can you say about the meaning of the selection? Give compliments about the writing.

- Now, think together about when the author used commas. What about using *and* to identify the end of the list?

If students have suggestions, ask permission from the author before executing the changes.

**SUM IT UP** To a class editing chart, add "Use commas to separate words in a series. Write the word *and* before the last word." (Example: *I like cats, dogs, and turtles.*)

Remember, writers use commas when writing words in a series.

> ### Making a Peanut Butter and Jelly Sandwich
>
> You need to get the peanut butter, jelly, two pieces of bread, and knife out. Spread the peanut butter on one piece of bread. Spread the jelly on top of the peanut butter. Put the other piece of bread on top of all of that. Cut the sandwich into pieces. Eat!

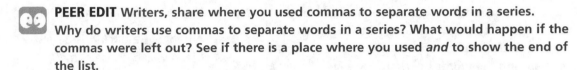

**DAY 3** | **Independent Practice**

Ask writers to look in their writing folders and select a piece of writing in which they used commas to separate words in a series. Give them a few minutes to reread for the use of commas to separate words in a series, and the use of the word *and* prior to the last item in the series.

**PEER EDIT** Writers, share where you used commas to separate words in a series. Why do writers use commas to separate words in a series? What would happen if the commas were left out? See if there is a place where you used *and* to show the end of the list.

**SUM IT UP** When writers write about several things in one sentence, they use commas to separate those things. Then they write the word *and* before the last item. This is called using commas in a series.

## ✅ Assess the Learning

- Provide writers with a photocopy of a sentence that has items in a series. Have students work independently to insert the commas. Assess understanding.

- Assess student use of commas in a series in the note to parents recommended in Link the Learning (below).

## 🔗 Link the Learning

- Have children describe a group of resources they have used in their learning and insert commas between items in the list. (Example: Today, in science, we used water, a pitcher, food coloring, and a flower to learn about how water travels up a stem.)

- Ask your media specialist to recommend read-aloud titles that demonstrate the use of commas to separate words in a series. *Cloudy With a Chance of Meatballs* by Judith Barrett has examples of phrases separated by commas in a series.

- Read *Song and Dance Man* by Karen Ackerman and search for a series connected by commas.

- Have children write notes to their parents, listing things they need for an outing, new learning they have encountered, or their favorite books.

# Quotation Marks: Dialogue

## DAY 1   Model the Focus Point

Today, I'm going to write a story about talking animals. As a writer, I need to use quotation marks to let the reader know that characters are talking. I'll tell who is talking by writing *asked Albert* or *replied Jane*. I put the quotation marks around the words the character says.

 **TURN AND TALK** Writers, consider the way I included dialogue. Where did I write the quotation marks? What other marks did I use, and where did they go? What words did I use instead of using *said*? How can you tell what is dialogue and what is narration?

**SUM IT UP** Remember, when including dialogue, surround the talking parts with quotation marks.

> **Modeled Writing Sample**
>
> Alfred was a duck. His best friend was a goose named Jane.
>
> "What should we do after school?" asked Alfred.
>
> "I don't know," replied Jane. "Should we go to the park?"
>
> "Absolutely!" grinned Alfred.

## DAY 2   Guided Practice

Display appendix page 186 or a student writing sample that includes dialogue. If the author is one of your students, invite the author to read the selection to the class.

 **TURN AND TALK**

- Writers, talk about a celebration you can offer the author. What can you say about the meaning of the selection? Give compliments about the writing.

- Now, think together about what the author did when the characters were talking. How did the author use quotation marks? Are they in the right place? Could we add quotation marks?

If students have suggestions, involve the author before executing the changes.

**SUM IT UP** To a class editing chart, add "Use quotation marks around dialogue. Quotation marks tell who is doing the talking."

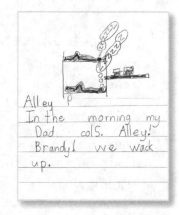

**DAY 3** | **Independent Practice**

Ask writers to look in their writing folders and select a piece of writing that includes dialogue or could have dialogue added to the text or the illustration. Give students a few minutes to reread for dialogue.

 **PEER EDIT** Share your thoughts about dialogue. Do you have some dialogue in your writing? Were you able to add some? How did you do at finding words other than *said* to tell who was talking?

 **SUM IT UP** Remember, when including dialogue, surround the talking parts with quotation marks.

 **Assess the Learning**

- Use a class record-keeping grid as you observe editors at work. Check off those students who use dialogue, identify the speaker, and use substitutes for *said*.

- Have individuals edit for punctuation in dialogue, after they have had multiple experiences working with a partner on typed familiar text with unpunctuated dialogue. Record your observations.

**Link the Learning**

- This is a perfect time to break out your favorite fiction selections and have children read to focus on dialogue. As they gain confidence, have partners take turns reading dialogue and narration, or form small groups to engage in a Readers Theater.

- Have children think about conversations they had at lunch or on the playground and write what they heard, using quotation marks.

- During writer's workshop, remind students how to include dialogue.

- Type familiar text with dialogue, omitting the punctuation. Have partners edit for punctuation.

- Model adding dialogue to an illustration to add humor and interest to the writing.

# Apostrophes: Contractions

**DAY 1**  **Model the Focus Point**

**Contractions are fun. They allow us to take two words and squish them into one shorter word. Let me show you.** (On a whiteboard, write *cannot*, and then erase the *no* and insert an apostrophe.) **I just made a contraction.** *Can't* **is short for** *cannot*. **The apostrophe is important because it shows the reader where the missing letter used to be. I am going to start writing—keep an eye out for those contractions! My first sentence is,** *I* do not *like getting up early*. **I can use a contraction. The short way to say** *do not* **is** *don't*. **Watch how I take out** *no* **and slip in the apostrophe so it now says** *don't*. **Cool!**

> **Modeled Writing Sample**
>
> I don't like getting up early. I shouldn't just lie there, but it feels so good! I wish morning wouldn't come so early in the day!

 **TURN AND TALK** Writers, consider the way I wrote contractions. What did I do when I made two words into one? What contractions can you think of?

 **SUM IT UP** Remember, when writers use contractions, they make two words into one by taking out letters and putting an apostrophe in their place. Contractions make our writing sound more like our talking.

**DAY 2**  **Guided Practice**

Display this example from appendix page 187 or a writing sample from a student. If the author is one of your students, invite the author to read the selection to the class.

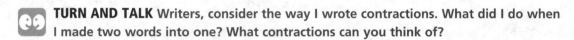

 **TURN AND TALK**

• **Writers, talk about a celebration you can offer the author. What can you say about the meaning of the selection? Give compliments about the writing.**

• **Now, think together about using contractions. Did the author write any contractions? Is the apostrophe in the correct place? Can you change the contraction back to two words? Which way sounds better to you? Why?**

If students have suggestions, ask permission from the author before executing the changes.

 **SUM IT UP** To a class editing chart, add "Use apostrophes to write contractions." (Example: *did not = didn't*)

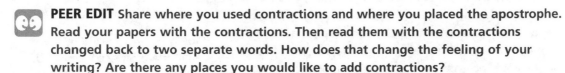

**DAY 3** | **Independent Practice**

Ask writers to look in their writing folders and select a piece of writing that includes contractions. Give them a few minutes to reread for contractions and the correct use of apostrophes.

**PEER EDIT** Share where you used contractions and where you placed the apostrophe. Read your papers with the contractions. Then read them with the contractions changed back to two separate words. How does that change the feeling of your writing? Are there any places you would like to add contractions?

**SUM IT UP** Remember, when writers use contractions, they make two words into one by taking out letters and putting an apostrophe in their place. Contractions make our writing sound more like our talking.

## ✓ Assess the Learning

- Use a class record-keeping grid as you observe editors at work. Check off those students who are writing contractions effectively.

- In small groups, have children use whiteboards to write out the contractions you say. Observe for the use of an apostrophe for omitted letters.

## ∞ Link the Learning

- During writer's workshop, remind students to use apostrophes when they write contractions.

- Provide whiteboards. Give students two words to write (e.g., "is not"), and then ask them to turn the words into a one-word contraction. (Examples: *are not, will not, I am, we are, have not*.)

- Those students who do not yet have this understanding can be gathered into a brief guided writing experience in which you might again model and guide them as they write contractions.

- Use children's literature that shows contractions, such as *Don't Let the Pigeon Drive the Bus* by Mo Willems.

# Apostrophes: Possessives

**DAY 1** | **Model the Focus Point**

When writers want to let readers know that something belongs to only one person, they add an apostrophe *s* to the end of the person's name. An apostrophe looks like a comma, but we write it above the line, not on the line. Now, it's your job to watch as I use an apostrophe *s* to show when something belongs to only one person, or one thing, or one place.

> **Modeled Writing Sample**
>
> Today is Mary's birthday. Her little brother's bike is red, but Mary's new bike is bright green. Way too cool!

Share your thinking about using an apostrophe to show singular possession for each example.

 **TURN AND TALK** Writers, consider the way I showed ownership. Where did I write the apostrophe? What letter did I add after the apostrophe to show ownership? Could I write, . . . *the dog's food?* or *The house's front door. . . ?* How many dogs was I writing about? How many houses? How did you know?

 **SUM IT UP** Remember, to show that one person, thing, or place owns something, simply add an *'s* to the end of the word.

**DAY 2** | **Guided Practice**

Display this example from appendix page 184 or a sample of student writing from your class. If the author is one of your students, invite the author to read the selection to the class.

 **TURN AND TALK**

- Writers, talk about a celebration you can offer the author. What can you say about the meaning of the selection? Give compliments about the writing.

- Now, think together about how the author showed that one person, thing, or place owned something. Did the author use an *'s* at the end of the word?

If students have suggestions, ask permission from the author before executing the changes.

 **SUM IT UP** To a class editing chart, add "Use an *'s* at the end of a person's, thing's, or place's name to show ownership." (Example: Mary's books)

Remember, writers can show ownership by using an *'s* at the end of the name of a person, thing, or place.

Ask writers to look in their writing folders and select a piece of writing in which they showed ownership by writing an *'s* at the end of someone's name. Give students a few minutes to reread for the use of *'s* at the end of a noun to show singular possessive nouns.

 **PEER EDIT** Share where you used an *'s* at the end of a name of a person, thing, or place. What were you showing by adding *'s*?

 **SUM IT UP** Remember, to show that one person, thing, or place owns something, simply add *'s* to the end of the word.

 **Assess the Learning**

- Have students illustrate and create a list of items in their home. They might list things such as Mom's apron, Dad's favorite chair, and Anna's skateboard. Assess their ability to use the possessive appropriately.

- Have students select a writing sample in which they used an apostrophe to show possession.

## Link the Learning

- During writer's workshop, remind students to use *'s* to show singular possession.

- Read literature with plenty of possessive apostrophes, such as *Lilly's Purple Plastic Purse* by Kevin Henkes, *Thomas' Snowsuit* by Robert Munsch, *Sister Anne's Hands* by Marybeth Lorbiecki, or a version of "Goldilocks and the Three Bears."

- In the classroom, label items with possessive labels: *Ann's backpack*, *Joshua's chair*, and so on.

# Cycles for Success With Capitalization

**A**s kindergarten and first-grade writers are often still learning to differentiate between capital and lowercase letters, we are not surprised when their fledgling drafts have a merry mix of lowercase letters and capitals. What we do need to do is help these young writers learn that they must reserve the use of capital letters for names and the beginning of sentences. As you review the lessons in this section, you will want to take special note of the lesson Use Mostly Lowercase Letters, as this is one that kindergarten and early first graders are sure to find helpful.

Capital letters transmit a message of "take notice, this word has special significance." This is important to emergent readers as they need all the help they can get in controlling volume and flow while they navigate letters and sounds. This is also important to emergent writers as they want to be understood and have others able to access their messages. Capital letters are helpful tools that clarify meaning.

We encourage you to pay special attention to using capital letters in names, as we all know how accessible names are to learners at this age. Then, during your modeled writing, think aloud about the use of capital letters and help writers discover that periods and capital letters make terrific partners as we create meaningful sentences.

# Use Mostly Lowercase Letters

**Model the Focus Point**

When writers first learn their letters, it takes a lot of thinking to remember how to make them. **Remember this: most words use ALL lowercase letters. Sometimes we use uppercase letters for special reasons. As I write, watch how I use mostly lowercase letters, and when I need to, I use uppercase letters.** (Keep the focus on the use of lowercase letters, but mention capitals at the beginning of sentences and for the word, *I.*) **I will start with a capital letter because all sentences start with a capital, but watch. The rest of my sentence will be all lowercase letters.** *I am hoping for...*

> **Modeled Writing Sample**
>
> I am hoping for a sunny day tomorrow. I bought some beautiful new plants but need to have the ground dry out just a bit. No rain, please!

 **TURN AND TALK** **Writers, think and talk together about when I used lowercase letters and when I used uppercase letters. Did I ever put a capital in the middle or end of a word? When I wrote a capital letter, where did it go?**

 **SUM IT UP** **Remember, writers usually write a word with all lowercase letters. They use capitals at the beginning of a word for special reasons.**

**DAY 2** **Guided Practice**

Display appendix page 172 or a sample from your students. If the author is one of your students, invite the author to read the selection to the class.

 **TURN AND TALK**
- **Writers, talk about a celebration you can offer the author. What can you say about the meaning of the selection? Give compliments about the writing.**

- **Think together about how the author used upper- and lowercase letters. Did the author use only lowercase letters in most words? What are some reasons for using capitals? Give examples.**

If students have suggestions, ask permission from the author before executing the changes.

 **SUM IT UP** To a class editing chart, add "Use only lowercase letters to write most words." (Examples: *car, boats*)

**Remember, writers, for most words we use all lowercase letters. We have special reasons when we use capital letters.**

**DAY 3** | **Independent Practice**

Ask writers to look in their writing folders and select a piece of writing. Give them a few minutes to reread their work to check if they used lowercase letters for most of their words. Provide access to an upper- and lowercase alphabet card to those who need the support. Did students find any words that needed a capital? Why? Encourage writers to edit their papers.

**PEER EDIT** Share your writing with your partner. Did you use lowercase letters for almost all of your words? Did you write your name? Did you use a capital letter to begin your name?

**SUM IT UP** Remember, writers usually write a word with all lowercase letters. They use capitals at the beginning of a word for special reasons, such as writing their names or beginning a sentence.

## ✔ Assess the Learning

- Gather writing samples and note which students are using lowercase letters and which ones are still inserting uppercase letters in inappropriate positions.

- During independent reading, have readers identify words that have all lowercase and words that have capitals. Have students explain why the letters are lower- or uppercase.

## Link the Learning

- Into a small group, gather those students who are still inserting uppercase letters, for additional support with handwriting and letter formation of lowercase letters.

- During small-group reading, have children place highlighter tape over uppercase letters and talk about how many letters are uppercase and when it is okay to switch from lowercase.

- During writer's workshop, remind students about the appropriate use of upper- and lowercase letters.

- Engage in an alphabet book study. Have writers create alphabet books in which decisions about lower- and uppercase letters abound. Not every page needs to be embellished with student writing. Some pages can simply include upper- and lowercase letters plus illustrations.

# Capitalize the Beginning of Sentences

 **DAY 1** **Model the Focus Point**

Writers always capitalize the first word of a sentence, no matter what kind of sentence it is. As I write, watch how I use a capital letter to begin every sentence. *Once I got the hiccups.* Do you see how I started my sentence? That is important. We need a capital letter every time we start a sentence.

**Modeled Writing Sample**

Once, I got the hiccups. They wouldn't stop. At first, it was funny. Then, it wasn't. They finally stopped, but I was worn out!

 **TURN AND TALK** Writers, put your heads together and count the number of sentences I wrote. How many of my sentences begin with a capital letter? Do any of my sentences begin with a lowercase letter?

 **SUM IT UP** Remember, a sentence always begins with a capital letter.

 **DAY 2** **Guided Practice**

Display appendix page 175 or a writing sample created by a student in your room. If the author is one of your students, invite the author to read the selection to the class.

**TURN AND TALK**
- Writers, talk about a celebration you can offer the author. What can you say about the meaning of the selection? Give compliments about the writing.

- Think together. Did the author use a capital at the beginning of every sentence? How did using a capital at the beginning of each sentence help you as a reader?

If students have suggestions, ask permission from the author before executing the changes.

**SUM IT UP** To a class editing chart, add "Begin every sentence with a capital letter." (Example: My cat is cute.)

**Remember, all writers use capitals to begin sentences.**

**DAY 3** Independent Practice

Ask writers to look in their writing folders and select a piece of writing. Give them a few minutes to reread and edit for the use of capital letters at the beginning of sentences.

 **PEER EDIT** Show your partner where you used a capital letter at the beginning of sentences. Share a place where you edited and added a capital letter to begin a sentence.

 **SUM IT UP** Remember, a sentence always begins with a capital letter.

 **Assess the Learning**

• Use a Class Record-Keeping Grid to identify students who are effectively using capital letters at the beginning of sentences.

• Provide students with a typed text of a familiar big book with capital letters omitted at the beginning of sentences. Have them proofread and edit for capitals at the beginning of the sentence.

**Link the Learning**

• During writer's workshop, remind students to use capitals to begin their sentences.

• During small-group reading instruction, give readers a few thin strips of sticky notes. Show them how to "flag" the first word in a sentence. After they finish flagging the first word in sentences, have partners discuss those important capital letters at the beginning of each sentence.

• During health or science, use a sentence strip to model and think aloud about writing content-based sentences. Emphasize capitalizing the first word. (Example: There are four seasons. I like fall.) Then have students do the same. Have partners share their writing, first for content and then for capitalization of the first word in a sentence.

• Invite partners to revisit familiar big books and put sticky notes on capital letters. Then have them meet with another partner pair and share their thinking about why the author used uppercase letters.

# Capitalize Proper Nouns: Names and Places

**DAY 1** | **Model the Focus Point**

People's names are so important that we always capitalize the first letter of a name. Names of particular places, like our school, are also capitalized. Today, I'll begin a class record-keeping grid with all of your names. Then, anyone who comes into our room will know whose classroom this is. (Come up with any authentic reason for writing students' names: in a list, on 3"x5" cards, and so on.) We'll call this list *Mrs. Darby's Class at Elmonica School*. Look at the capitals I used in just the title. Let's count them. Wow! I just used a lot of names in one line.

> **Modeled Writing Sample**
>
> Mrs. Darby's Class at Elmonica School
>
> Kevin Furlong
>
> Linda Miller
>
> Condido Aboitiz

 **TURN AND TALK** Writers, look over my writing. Did I capitalize each person's first and last names? If I wrote people's middle names, would I need to capitalize them, too? What else was capitalized?

 **SUM IT UP** Remember, writers always capitalize the first letter of people's names and the names of particular places, like (our school's name, _____).

**DAY 2** | **Guided Practice**

Display a writing sample from a student in your room or use appendix page 183. If the author is one of your students, invite the author to read the selection to the class.

 **TURN AND TALK**

- Writers, talk about a celebration you can offer the author. What can you say about the meaning of the selection? Give compliments about the writing.

- Think together about capitalizing the first letter of people's names and the names of particular places. Were all the people's names capitalized?

If students have suggestions, ask permission from the author before executing the changes.

 **SUM IT UP** To a class editing chart, add "Capitalize the first letter of people's names or names of particular places." (Examples: Mary Brown and Elmonica School)

Remember, writers capitalize people's names and the name of a particular place.

**DAY 3** | **Independent Practice**

Ask writers to look at their writing folders and select a piece of writing that includes someone's name or the name of a particular place. Give students a few minutes to reread for capitalizing the first letter of a person's name or a particular place.

 **PEER EDIT** Share with your partner where you capitalized people's names. If you wrote about a particular place, check to see if you capitalized that, too.

 **SUM IT UP** Remember, writers always capitalize the first letter of people's names and the names of particular places, like (your school's name).

## ✓ Assess the Learning

- Confer with individuals to identify which students differentiate between capitalizing a name and the first word in a sentence.

- Assess writing samples that include proper nouns, and record observations about capitalization.

##  Link the Learning

- Add student photographs or self-portraits next to their names to create a writing reference for letters and sounds. Encourage children to use each other's names in their writing.

- During shared reading, identify names for people and places and point out the capital letters.

- Visit the office and show children the name of the principal on the door.

- Ask the custodian if your writers can tour the storeroom to search for packaging that has the names of companies.

- During guided reading, search for names in books and notice the capital letters.

# Capitalize Days of the Week

**DAY 1** Model the Focus Point

Words that need to begin with a capital letter, like our names, are called proper nouns. Another group of proper nouns that need a beginning capital letter are the days of the week. Watch how I use a capital to begin each day of the week. Now that I've finished, watch how I reread to see if it makes sense and sounds right. Now, watch me reread to make sure that I capitalized the first letter each time I wrote a day of the week.

> **Modeled Writing Sample**
>
> There are seven days in every week. I like Saturday morning because I get things done. I like Saturday night because I can relax. Is your favorite day Saturday, too?

 **TURN AND TALK** Writers, put your heads together and think about capitalizing the first letter of each day of the week. Did I do that? Which day of the week did I write about? If I had written about Monday or Friday, would I still have needed to capitalize the first letter? Why? Did I capitalize the word *day*? Why?

 **SUM IT UP** Remember, always capitalize the beginning letter when writing the days of the week.

**DAY 2** Guided Practice

Use appendix page 181 or select a student writing sample that includes a day of the week. If the author is one of your students, invite the author to read the selection to the class.

> **Saturday at the Park**
>
> It snowed on Saturday. We goed to the park. It was beautiful! I wanted to stay forever. It lookt like winter. We goded home before it got dark.

 **TURN AND TALK**
- Writers, talk about a celebration you can offer the author. What can you say about the meaning of the selection? Give compliments about the writing.

- Now, think together about beginning the days of the week with a capital letter. Did the author always use a beginning capital letter?

If students have suggestions, ask permission from the author before executing the changes.

 **SUM IT UP** To a class editing chart add "Capitalize the first letter of the days of the week." (Example: **M**onday)

Remember, writers capitalize the first letter of the days of the week.

**DAY 3** Independent Practice

Ask writers to look in their writing folders and select a piece of writing that includes the days of the week. Give them a few minutes to reread for capitalizing the days of the week.

 **PEER EDIT** Share with your partner which day of the week you wrote about. Explain why you wrote about that day. Did you capitalize the first letter of the day of the week?

 **SUM IT UP** Remember, always capitalize the beginning letter when writing the days of the week.

## ✔ Assess the Learning

- Provide opportunities for students to write an innovation of *The Very Hungry Caterpillar* by Eric Carle so they have an authentic purpose to write about the days of the week. Meet with individuals to assess for placement of capitals for days of the week.

- Have students write about their two favorite days of the week and why they like them. Assess for capitalization.

##  Link the Learning

- Have students write letters to their parents, telling their favorite things to do each day of the week.

- Provide students with a list of the days of the week and a blank calendar form of the upcoming month. Have them complete the form, focusing on using a capital letter to begin the days of the week, and then keep the calendar on their desk and enjoy having a personal calendar for the month.

- Have students include the day of the week, in addition to their name and the date, on the top of their papers.

- Read *Tuesday* by David Wiesner.

# Capitalize Titles

## DAY 1　Model the Focus Point

When we write a title of a book or a title for the stories we write, we need to use capital letters to begin most of the words in the titles. We always capitalize the important words. The little words such as *a*, *and*, or *the* are not capitalized, unless they are the first word of the title. Watch how I capitalize most of the words in titles as I write a list of books I plan to read to the class.

 **TURN AND TALK** Writers, think about the ways I use capitals when I write book titles. What would you tell other students to do when they write book titles? If you wrote a story and gave it a title, which words would you capitalize? Which words would you keep lowercase?

 **SUM IT UP** When writing the title of a book or a title for our stories, use capitals to begin most of the words in titles. We always capitalize the first, last, and any other important words.

> **Modeled Writing Sample**
>
> Books I want to read or reread to the class are:
>
> *Alexander and the Terrible, Horrible, No Good, Very Bad Day*
>
> *Frog and Toad*
>
> *The Three Little Pigs*

## DAY 2　Guided Practice

Use the writing sample from appendix page 181 or a writing sample from your class. If there is a title present, talk about capitalization. If there is no title, have the class create one, and add the title on the overhead transparency. If the author is one of your students, invite the author to read the selection to the class

 **TURN AND TALK**

- Writers, talk about a celebration you can offer the author. What can you say about the meaning of the selection? Give compliments about the writing.

- Now, think together about using capitals in titles. Did the author follow the rules for using capitals? What are those rules?

If students have suggestions, ask permission from the author before executing the changes.

 **SUM IT UP** To a class editing chart add "Capitalize the first, last, and any other important words in titles." (Example: *Frog and Toad*)

Remember, writers capitalize most of the words in a book title or in their own story titles.

**DAY 3** | **Independent Practice**

Ask writers to look over the titles in their writing folders. Do they have titles for all of their work? Did they use capital letters? Did they ever include book titles in their writing? Give them a few minutes to reread for the use of capitals in book titles or their own story titles.

 **PEER EDIT** Show each other where you used capitals when writing book titles or your own story titles.

 **SUM IT UP** When writing the title of a book or a title for their stories, writers use capitals to begin most of the words in titles. They always capitalize the first, last, and any other important words.

## ✔ Assess the Learning

- Have children create a list of their favorite books. Assess their lists for an understanding of capitalization in a title.

- Review writing folders to see how students are doing with capitalizing titles in their writing.

## Link the Learning

- Provide each student with a sticky note to record the title of a book recommended for a read-aloud. Cluster recommendations by title on the blackboard.

- Have each child collect four favorite books from guided reading, read-aloud, shared, or independent reading. Then have partners look at the books together and talk about how each book handles capitalizing the title.

- Work with the students to create titles for charts in the classroom.

- Have student authors create titles for bulletin boards and label areas in the classroom.

# Pulling It All Together

For learning to be long-lasting, children need opportunities to explore their understandings in more than one context. The Power Burst Lessons and Pulling It All Together Cycles are designed to provide interactive experiences in which children can review conventions and mechanics they have recently explored in a cycle. These experiences are not designed to teach new content, but rather to review and support the transfer of learning to other contexts.

There are two parts to this section:

**Power Burst Lessons:** These are learning experiences that fit nicely into small windows of time. When you have ten minutes, slip in one of these interactive experiences and review recently addressed conventions and mechanics.

**Pulling It All Together Cycles:** These are fully developed cycles that are linked to the Yearlong Planner and designed to tie together multiple points of learning. These cycles are designed to provide intensive review of three weeks of learning within the context of an authentic writing purpose that has a real audience.

# Power Burst Lesson: Secret Sentences

For secret sentences, place each word and punctuation mark for a familiar sentence onto individual sheets of paper. Then teams of students (each child holding one card) move themselves around to arrange their sentence into an order that makes sense. Learners check to be sure their sentence begins with a capital letter, that there is end punctuation, and that there is a space between each word.

With kindergarten and early first grade, begin with sentences from much-loved picture books or big books. It helps to choose lines from treasured selections, such as "In went the pig, wishy-washy, wishy-washy" or "Don't let the pigeon drive the bus!" These familiar lines energize conversations and enable children to navigate the sentences with confidence. As they gain experience with Secret Sentences, you may want to branch out to sentences that are less familiar but are structured to provide a review of recently learned mechanics and conventions.

As confidence grows, children enjoy working in partner pairs to create their own Secret Sentences for others to assemble.

# Power Burst Lesson: Scavenger Hunt

Using a big book, demonstrate how to survey the book to look for periods, capital letters, spaces between words, and so on. Select a convention or mechanic you have worked on in a recent cycle and count to see how many times it occurs in the big book.

Once children catch on to the Scavenger Hunt idea, have individuals, partners, or teams survey picture books, big books, guided reading selections, weekly newsmagazines, and so on, keeping a tally of their findings. As they continue to mature in conducting Scavenger Hunts with differing purposes, you may want to have them work with partners to conduct a Scavenger Hunt through their own writing folders.

# Power Burst Lesson: Cut Up Sentences

Select a sentence from a highly familiar picture book and write it on a sentence strip with no spaces between the words. Show the children the original page from the book, touching the words as you read. Then show them the sentence strip and explain how difficult it is to read the sentence when there are no spaces. Use scissors to separate the words and place them in a pocket chart so children can observe that the sentence is now much easier to read.

Demonstrate the process with several reading selections. When students show they are ready, provide them with photocopies of sentences with no spaces; then have partners work together to separate the words. If the sentences are prepared on a computer, be sure to use a very large font and type size so the individual words are large enough to handle easily.

# Power Burst Lesson: Cloze With Big Books

Cloze techniques can be helpful for reviewing a wide range of conventions and mechanics.

**End-punctuation example:** For a review of end punctuation, place sticky notes over the end punctuation in a familiar big book. As you enjoy rereading the book, have children turn and talk every time you come to a sticky note and decide if you are most likely to reveal a period, a question mark, or an exclamation point.

Just then, the three pigs heard
a bump
and a thump
Something was scraping
the side of the house

**Past-tense-verb example:** Cover *-ed* endings to verbs and talk about how the sentence sounds. Then uncover the endings and read again to celebrate what you noticed about past-tense verbs!

So the wolf huff___
and he puff___
and he puff___
and he huff___
But he **couldn't** blow the house in!

# Power Burst Lesson: Cloze for High-Frequency Words in Writing

Place this text or one you have constructed on the overhead or on a chart. Read the selection and explain that the words in the blanks are words that are used a lot in writing, so it is important to learn how to spell them. Have partners work with whiteboards to attempt to spell the words, and then show them how you can go to the word wall to check the spelling before placing the word into the passage.

One _____ it snowed.

Mommy _____

I rolled a big snowball.

We _____ a snowman! Then Mommy

pulled me _____ a sled. But I fell

_____. I lost my glove and I

_____ cold. So we _____ indoors.

I hope the snow is _____ tomorrow.

# Power Burst Lesson: Oh No! Oh Yes!

This lesson is designed to focus children on grammatical structures in a playful way. This experience should be reserved for after the cycles in the grammar section of this resource. Each time you share this lesson with children, focus on only one grammatical feature at a time to avoid confusion.

First, arrange children in pairs and give each pair cards that say:

| Oh No! | Oh Yes! |
|:------:|:-------:|

Next, make a statement such as "I goed to the store" and think aloud for the children, explaining that grown-ups wouldn't say it that way. Instead, they would say, "I went to the store." Have partners try the sentence the wrong way and hold up the "Oh, No!" sign. Have them say it the correct way and hold up the "Oh, Yes!" sign. Continue playing with sentences that the children can talk about and respond to with their signs.

Examples to consider:

|  | Oh No! | Oh Yes! |
|---|---|---|
| Complete Sentences | Anna went | Anna went to the park. |
|  | My puppy | My puppy is getting big. |
| Single vs. Double Subject | My mother, she went to the store. | My mother went to the store. |
|  | My brother, he flew his kite. | My brother flew his kite. |
| Pronoun Order | Me and my sister ate popcorn. | My sister and I ate popcorn. |
|  | I and my brother love to play soccer. | My brother and I love to play soccer. |

# Pulling It All Together Cycle #1: Signs to Label the Classroom

Stretching Out Words • Use a Picture Alphabet Card • Name on Paper

## DAY 1  Model Writing for an Audience

I have been noticing that we are missing opportunities to add writing to our room! We need signs in our classroom. In our school, we have signs that say "office," tell room numbers, and show which bathroom to use. I am looking at our classroom and thinking of signs I can create. I am going to make a sign that says *paper towels* to place on the towel dispenser. Listen as I stretch out the words *paper* and *towel*. I hear *p-a-p-r* I will use my picture alphabet card to help me find the letters I need. I will stretch out *towel* and write that, too. I hear *t-l*. Next, I need to add my name. Watch how I write my name in small letters at the bottom of the sentence strip.

> **Modeled Writing Sample**
>
> Papr Tl
>
> Mrs. Hoyt

The whole idea of a sign is that others will read it. I need to reread and check my work. I am going to make sure I added my name and stretched out my words to add all the letters I can. Good writers do that.

**TURN AND TALK** Writers, talk about the sign I made. Can you read it? Did I use enough letters to help you understand? What did you see me doing? What will you need to do if you want to make a sign? Who can tell me what steps we need to follow?

**CREATE AUTHENTIC PURPOSE** Have children work in pairs to create signs to place around the classroom. Remind them to stretch out words, use their alphabet cards, and then write their names. Be sure they pause to reread and check their work before posting their signs.

**ASSESS THE LEARNING** As students create their signs, observe closely and create a list of those students who need additional small–group support to stretch out words and to use their alphabet cards.

**SUM IT UP** Writers! Look at all of our signs. Let's think together about what we know how to do: We can stretch words out and listen to sounds. We can use alphabet cards. We reread to check our work. We also know good editors write their names on their papers! Hooray for us!

## DAY 2  Guided Practice

**MODEL: TRANSFER LEARNING TO ANOTHER CONTEXT** While children watch, demonstrate selecting a piece from a writing folder and using the steps on the class editing chart to check the writing. As you reread the writing, think out loud about stretching words, using the alphabet card, and rereading to check for a name.

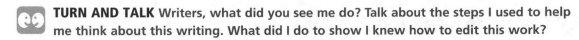 **TURN AND TALK** Writers, what did you see me do? Talk about the steps I used to help me think about this writing. What did I do to show I knew how to edit this work?

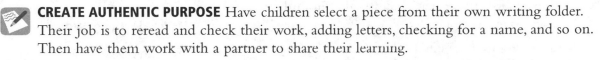 **CREATE AUTHENTIC PURPOSE** Have children select a piece from their own writing folder. Their job is to reread and check their work, adding letters, checking for a name, and so on. Then have them work with a partner to share their learning.

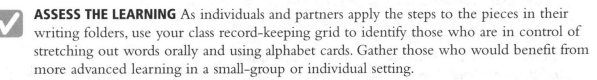 **ASSESS THE LEARNING** As individuals and partners apply the steps to the pieces in their writing folders, use your class record-keeping grid to identify those who are in control of stretching out words orally and using alphabet cards. Gather those who would benefit from more advanced learning in a small-group or individual setting.

**SUM IT UP** Look how we are growing as writers. We created signs and remembered to stretch out words and use our alphabet cards. We also reread work in our writing folders. We are terrific editors, aren't we!

## DAY 3  Support and Extend the Learning

Select experiences that will best support your learners:

- Model making signs to place around the school, within the gymnasium, on the playground, or in the library. As on Day 1, demonstrate stretching words, using alphabet cards, and checking for names. Have children work with partners to create and post their signs around the school.

- After a read-aloud experience, ask students to help you stretch out some of the most important words that were in the story. After *Mrs. Wishy Washy*, you might model stretching out *pig, duck, wishy, washy,* or *mud*. Show the children how you stretch words out and use the alphabet card. Have partners think of favorite words from the story to stretch out and write on sentence strips. Have them sign their names.

- Model writing a summary of an experience at school. As you write, be very explicit as you stretch out words and use an alphabet card. Then be sure to write your name.

- Those who do not yet demonstrate independence in placing their names on their work, stretching out words, or using an alphabet card can be gathered into brief guided writing experiences in which you might again model these important processes in a small-group setting.

- Continuously model the importance of touching each word during rereading.

- Ask permission to have students create signs for the office, signs that welcome visitors, signs that provide instructions on picking up students, and so on.

# Pulling It All Together Cycle #2:
# From the Desk of _____ Notes

Big Words/Little Words • Keep Letters in a Word Together • Reread to Add Letters

### DAY 1  Model Writing for an Audience

Note: Prepare large paper that replicates the From the Desk of ___ note page (see appendix page 162).

**I am going to write a note to __** (name another teacher). **I want to tell her about the great book we read yesterday because I think she might want to read it, too.** (Begin drafting.) **As I write, I am going to think about big words and little words so I can remember which ones need more letters. I want to tell about** *Have You Seen My Duckling?* **I know** *My* **will be a short word with just two letters.** *Duckling* **is going to be longer and have more letters. As I write, watch how I keep the letters in each word close together so I know they are part of the same word.** (after drafting) **Now, I need to think about rereading. That is what writers do. I want to reread first to be sure it makes sense. Next, I reread to see if I can stretch words and add more letters to my words. Finally, I can check to be sure I put my name on the paper!**

> **Modeled Writing Sample**
>
> From the Desk of <u>Mrs. Hoyt</u>
>
> I read <u>Have You Seen My Duckling</u>. I really liked the mother duck. She looked for a long time to find her baby.

**TURN AND TALK Writers, talk about the note I wrote. What did you see me doing? If you were going to write a note to take home, what book could you write about?**

**CREATE AUTHENTIC PURPOSE** Provide students with copies of the From the Desk of _____ notes on page 162. Have them write a note to take home, telling about their favorite book. Remind them to think about big words that need more letters, keeping letters together, and rereading to add letters to words. After drafting, have partners read their notes to each other.

**ASSESS THE LEARNING** As students create their notes, identify those students who need additional small-group support to stretch out words, identify large and small words, reread to add letters, or write their names.

**SUM IT UP Writers! We have written so many wonderful notes. Let's think together about what we know how to do. We can stretch words out and listen to sounds. We can reread to add more letters. We can keep letters in a word close together. Hooray for us!**

## DAY 2 | Guided Practice

**MODEL: TRANSFER LEARNING TO ANOTHER CONTEXT** Model how to select a piece from a writing folder and show children how you can reread a piece of writing. Think aloud about stretching out words, rereading to add letters, using an picture alphabet card to think about sounds, keeping letters close together, and writing your name as you examine a piece from the folder.

 **TURN AND TALK** Writers, what did you see me do? Talk about the way I reread the writing. Which steps are you getting really good at?

 **CREATE AUTHENTIC PURPOSE** Have children look at their own writing folder to select a piece to reread. Encourage them to think about looking at letters and the ways they are grouped. Be sure their picture alphabet cards are close at hand as they attempt to add more letters and think about sounds. Then have partners share their learning and any changes they were able to make.

 **ASSESS THE LEARNING** As individuals and partners reread the pieces in their writing folders, use your class record-keeping grid to identify those who are in control of each step and would benefit from more advanced learning in a small-group or individual setting.

 **SUM IT UP** Look how we are growing as writers. We wrote notes and reread pieces in our writing folders. We can remember to stretch out words, reread to add more letters, write our names, and use an picture alphabet card. Editors, give yourselves a big round of applause!

## DAY 3 | Support and Extend the Learning

Select experiences that will best support your learners:

- Play the Big Word/Little Word game. Explain to children that you are going to say words in pairs. One word will be a "big word" that needs a lot of letters. One word will be a "small word" that doesn't use so many letters. After students say the word pairs, their job is to tell their partner which word will need more letters!

- Create sentences using the names of children in class, such as *Anna likes swim, Pedro likes to run*, and *Tamika likes to sing*. (Placing a photo of the child in the sentence will assist with recognition of the names.) Cut the sentences apart in front of children and show them how the spaces between the words help you see the word boundaries. Push the words too tightly together and have volunteers move them apart again. As children become more proficient, cut one word into letters, push the letters far apart, and then arrange them back into a word.

- Model writing a summary of the day at school. As you write, be very explicit as you stretch out words and show children how to pause, listen to the word, and think about sounds to put on paper. Think aloud about which words are bigger and will need more letters or about clustering letters in a word so you can tell where each word ends. Model how you reread the piece, adding letters and adjusting your writing as you reread. Then, be sure to write your name!

- Hold an picture alphabet card, such as the one on appendix page 158, as you create a piece of writing. Show children how you stretch out a word and use the card to help you think of the letters you need to write.

# Pulling It All Together Cycle #3: Sticky Note Book Reviews

Counting the Words in Your Message • Use the Entire Page • Reread and Touch Each Word

## DAY 1 Model Writing for An Audience

Sticky note book reviews are terrific ways to find out what other people think of our favorite books. To write a sticky note book review, I think about a book I have read. If I liked it a lot, I will give it five stars and tell why. If I didn't like it, I will give it only one or two stars and tell why. *Are You My Mother?* by P. D. Eastman is a book. I like it very much because it has a happy ending. On my review I will give it four stars (****) and write *It has a happy ending!* Use your fingers and help me count the words. Now I need to look at the size of my sticky note. I am going to make my stars kind of small so there is enough room for my writing. I need to think about using the entire space. Now that I am finished, I will reread and touch each word. Good writers always check their work! Finally, I will place my review inside the cover of the book so someone else can read what I wrote.

**TURN AND TALK** Writers, talk about my sticky note book review. What did I do as a writer? Think together. What book could you review?

**CREATE AUTHENTIC PURPOSE** Have children work in partners to write sticky note book reviews of books from read-alouds, shared reading, small-group instruction, and independent experiences with books. Encourage them to reread as editors before placing their reviews into the books.

**ASSESS THE LEARNING** As students create their reviews, observe closely and create a list of those students who need additional small-group support to notice spaces between words, count the words in a message, think about the page, and use space wisely.

**SUM IT UP** Writers, look at all of our sticky note book reviews. What fun to get ideas from each other about our books! Writers, think together about what we know how to do: We can write sticky note book reviews. We can leave spaces between words, count the words we want to write, and use the whole paper!

## DAY 2 Guided Practice

**MODEL: TRANSFER LEARNING TO ANOTHER CONTEXT** Gather a collection of modeled writings you have done for children. Select one to reread and edit. Deliberately look at the class editing chart. Then have students observe as you reread and think aloud about leaving space between words, counting the words in the message, and considering the use of space on the page. Try to find a place where you can refine the writing by adding letters, words, or a space-filling illustration so the students can watch you adjust the piece.

 **TURN AND TALK** Writers, what did you see me do? Talk about the steps I used to reread my work. How will doing this help me be a better writer?

 **CREATE AUTHENTIC PURPOSE** Have children look at their own writing folder to select a piece to review. Encourage them to use the class editing chart and to feel free to add letters or adjust their work while they think about the page. Have them prepare to share their learning with a partner.

 **ASSESS THE LEARNING** As individuals and partners reread and rethink the pieces in their writing folders, use your class record-keeping grid to identify those who are in control of each step and would benefit from more advanced learning in a small-group or individual setting.

 **SUM IT UP** Look how we are growing as writers. We created sticky note book reviews and looked at our writing folders to practice leaving spaces between words, counting the words in a message, and using the whole page. Editors, look how much we know how to do!

## DAY 3 Support and Extend the Learning

Select experiences that will best support your learners:

- Have children continue making sticky note book reviews to share their thinking about books and create a sense of audience for writing. Encourage them to ask each other questions about the reviews they write.

- Take a tongue depressor and glue on two of the wiggly eyes you can purchase at craft stores, and then add a smile and a pom-pom to create a Mr. Spacey! Use Mr. Spacey after reading a familiar big book and show children how Mr. Spacey can fit between words on the page. Authors of published books leave spaces, too!

- Write a familiar sentence on sentence strips, and then cut the words apart. Place the words into a pocket chart, jamming the words tightly together so there are no spaces. Think aloud in front of children about how hard it is to read the sentence. Then count the words you want to say and show them how separating the words makes reading easier.

- Gather an array of big books and picture books and show children pages where the authors have used space in interesting ways. (Be sure to include some nonfiction.) Model a piece of writing on chart paper, in which you think aloud about space. Look at the page and think aloud about how you will arrange your illustration and writing. Then invite children to share the thinking in a shared writing experience. You control the pen; they provide the ideas and thinking.

- Those who do not yet demonstrate independence in leaving spaces between words may benefit from having a Mr. Spacey on hand while they write. Placing Mr. Spacey after every word ensures that there is enough space before starting the next word.

- Enlarge pages from familiar leveled books and have children cut the words apart. Have them count the number of words, push words apart so there are spaces, scramble them, and put them back together.

# Pulling It All Together Cycle #4: Thank-You Letters

Using Capital Letters • Periods • Rereading for Each Editing Point

**DAY 1** | **Model Writing for an Audience**

I am going to write a thank-you note to Mrs. _____, our cook. I want to thank her for the great cookies we had the other day. We know that when we write names we start with a capital letter. I will start my note, *Dear Mrs. ___.* Watch where I put the capital letters in her name. Now I am going to say, *Thank you for the delicious cookies. I got six chocolate chips in mine. Mmmm. Good!* Notice how I started each sentence with a capital letter and ended each sentence with a period. Let's count and see how many capital letters and periods I used. Now I am going to be a good editor. I will reread to check my work. I am rereading first to see if I used capital letters for names. Now, I will reread again to check for capitals at the beginning of each sentence. Finally, I will reread to check for periods at the end of each sentence.

> **Modeled Writing Sample**
>
> Dear Mrs. _____,
>
> Thank you for the delicious cookies. I got six chocolate chips in mine. Mmmm. Good!
>
> Your friend,
>
> Mrs. Hoyt

**TURN AND TALK** Writers, talk about the note I wrote to the cook. What did you see me doing? Why did I use capital letters? Did you notice my periods? How many did I use? What did you see me doing when I reread?

**CREATE AUTHENTIC PURPOSE** Have students write a note to someone, thanking that person for something. Remind them to use capital letters for names and sentence beginnings as well as to insert periods. Provide an opportunity for writers to share their notes with a partner and then deliver them.

**ASSESS THE LEARNING** As students create their notes, identify those students who need additional small-group support to use capital letters for names and at the beginning of sentences.

**SUM IT UP** Writers! We have written so many wonderful notes to the cook and to our parents. Let's think together about what we know how to do. We can use capital letters for names. We can use capital letters to start a sentence. We can use periods, too! Writers, stand up and clap for your wonderful learning!

## DAY 2    Guided Practice

**MODEL: TRANSFER LEARNING TO ANOTHER CONTEXT** Select a modeled writing you completed on a previous day. Read it aloud to ensure that everyone remembers the content. Then tell children you are going to reread the piece and think like an editor. Cut slim strips of brightly colored sticky notes to use in marking up your writing. Read once to identify proper names. Each time you find one, place a strip of sticky note over the capital letter and remind children of why it is a capital. Reread the piece and mark capitals at the beginning of sentences. Reread a third time to mark the periods. Celebrate your good thinking as a writer and, by all means, as you reread, add to the piece to model that good writers are constantly rethinking and revising their words.

 **TURN AND TALK** Writers, what did you see me do? Talk about the way I reread my writing. Why did I use capitals? How many periods did you count? How did my sticky notes help me think about my work?

 **CREATE AUTHENTIC PURPOSE** Have children look through their writing folders to select a piece to reread and mark with sticky-note strips. Have them reread completely for each focus point: capitals in proper names, capitals at the beginning of sentences, and periods at the end. Have partners share their marked-up texts with each other.

 **ASSESS THE LEARNING** As individuals and partners reread the pieces in their writing folders, use your class record-keeping grid to identify those who are in control of capitals and periods and would benefit from more advanced learning in a small-group or individual setting.

 **SUM IT UP** Look how we are growing as writers. We wrote notes and reread pieces in our writing folders. We can remember to use capital letters for specific purposes and use periods, too! Turn and tell your partner why you like using periods and capital letters.

## DAY 3    Support and Extend the Learning

Select experiences that will best support your learners:

- Create sentences using the names of children in class such as *Armando likes to run* and *Peyton likes to sing.* Write the strips without using capital letters or periods. Cut the words apart and place in a pocket chart. Read the sentences straight through with no pause between the sentences and ask children to help you think of where to place the periods and capital letters. Use extra sentence strips to insert punctuation and capitals.

- Create a piece of writing on sentence strips that has the capital letters in inappropriate places, such as in the middle of a word. Guide the children in reading the sentences and talking about how to use capital letters correctly. Use sentence strips to correct the use of capital/lowercase letters.

- Lay acetate over a big book and have students use a washable marker to identify capital letters and periods in the book. See page 10 for a graphic.

- Engage children in a Punctuation Scavenger Hunt through various favorite books. See page 18 for a graphic.

- During small-group instruction, have students identify capital letters and periods and talk about why they were used in the selection.

# Pulling It All Together Cycle #5: Danger! Signs

Exclamation Points • Touching Each Word While Proofreading • Keeping Letters In a Word Close Together

## DAY 1 Model Writing for an Audience

Today, we are going to make signs for our classroom that help us think about safety and being careful around dangerous things. For example, the heater can get really hot when the furnace is running so I am going to make a sign that says, *Danger, this heater gets very hot!* Notice how I use an exclamation to show that this is important. That exclamation means I am really serious about this. I am going to make a sign to place near our scissors, too. That sign will say, *Danger! Beware of sharp scissors!* These signs are important to help everyone stay safe, so I want to be sure others can read what I wrote. I need to reread my signs, touching each word to be sure I wrote all the words I needed. I am also going to check and make sure I kept the letters in each word close together. I really want everyone to be able to read these important signs.

> **Modeled Writing Sample**
>
> Danger, this heater gets very hot!
>
> Danger! Beware of sharp scissors!

**TURN AND TALK** Writers, talk about the danger signs I made. Why is it important for me to use an exclamation point? If you were going to make a danger sign, what would you want to mark as dangerous? Where would you put the exclamation point? Look at my letters. Can you tell which letters go together for each of my words?

**CREATE AUTHENTIC PURPOSE** Have students work in pairs to create danger signs for situations in the classroom or in the school. Encourage them to think together about where they could use exclamation points and to make sure the letters in each word stay close together. Be sure writers reread their work, touching each word before posting their signs.

**ASSESS THE LEARNING** As students create their danger signs, identify those students who need additional small-group support to touch each word during rereading and to use exclamation points.

**SUM IT UP** Writers! We have made some terrific danger signs to help everyone stay safe. Let's think together about what we know how to do: We can use exclamation points. We can reread and touch our words. We can keep letters in each word close together. Hooray for us!

## DAY 2 Guided Practice

**MODEL: TRANSFER LEARNING TO ANOTHER CONTEXT** Select a modeled writing completed on a previous day. Reread it and think aloud about exclamation points. How might the addition of exclamation points make the piece more interesting? Could you add sound words like *Plip, plop, crash, kerplunk, shhhh?* Could you add a sentence that needs an exclamation point at the end, such as *Oh no! I watched in horror as the glue starting running across the paper!* Share your thinking about exclamation points as you reread; then have the children watch as you add exclamation points, sound words, and so on. Finally, show them how, as a writer, you need to reread and touch each word to be sure you have all the words you need.

 **TURN AND TALK** Writers, what did you see me do with exclamation points? How did the exclamation points help my writing and make it more interesting? How could you use more exclamation points in your writing?

 **CREATE AUTHENTIC PURPOSE** Have children look at their own writing folder to select a piece to reread and insert exclamation points. Encourage them to think about adding sound words or words to show excitement, like *Look out!* Remind them to reread when they think they are finished, and touch each word. Finally, have partners share their learning and any exclamation points they were able to add.

 **ASSESS THE LEARNING** As individuals and partners reread the pieces in their writing folders, use your class record-keeping grid to identify those who are in control of exclamation points and touching words during a reread. These learners may benefit from more advanced learning in a small-group or individual setting.

 **SUM IT UP** Hooray for exclamation points! They make our writing more interesting. We made danger signs, reread pieces in our writing folders, and used a lot of exclamation points, didn't we? We also remembered to touch every word when we reread our work. Editors, give yourselves a big round of applause!

## DAY 3 | Support and Extend the Learning

Select experiences that will best support your learners:

- Create a celebration of exclamation points by gathering favorite read-alouds and shared reading selections that use exclamation points. Read and celebrate each time you find one.

- During shared reading or small-group reading instruction, use sticky notes to add speech bubbles to the pictures, with words a character might say and exclamation points. For example, in *Mrs. Wishy Washy*, a speech bubble near the pig might say, *Run! Here she comes again!*

- Model writing about something exciting that happened in class. Use sound words and lots of exclamation points to show excitement in the summary.

- Have students do an Exclamation Point Scavenger Hunt by rereading lots of favorite books from read-alouds, shared reading, and independent reading to search for exclamation points. Encourage them to use sticky notes to add exclamation points in places they think they would work.

- Gather into a small, guided group for students who need extra support in touching words as they reread their writing.

- Read Mo Willems books to celebrate the punctuation marks he uses.

- Provide dollar-store sunglasses and encourage writers to read with "new eyes" as they reread and touch words, looking for ways to add to their writing. See page 23 for a photograph.

# Pulling It All Together Cycle #6: Summarize a Science Experiment

Write a Sentence • Use Transition Words • Use the Word Wall

## DAY 1   Model Writing for an Audience

I am going to write and draw about the experiment we did in science. We have been invited to the class next door to share our writing and our experiment! Our learning will have an important audience. I have large paper divided into four boxes. Notice the boxes say *First, Next, Then,* and *Finally*. I know that *First, Anna placed food coloring in jars of water*. I can draw and write about that in Box #1. Let's check to see if I wrote a sentence. Did I tell <u>who</u> did something? Did I tell <u>what</u> was done? Good! The words I wrote told who and what, so I can put a period. That is a sentence. Box 2 has the word *Next*. I am thinking, *Next, a white flower* Is this a sentence? Did I tell who? Did I tell what happened? No, that won't work. Let's try, *Next, Michael placed a white flower in each jar*. How is that? (Continue writing, thinking aloud about complete sentences and transition words.) It is time to reread and check my work. Did I write complete sentences? Did I use *first, next, then, finally* to show order? Now, I need to use the word wall and check my spelling. I think *each* is on the wall. I will check that first. (Remove your writing from view so children do not attempt to copy it.)

> **Modeled Writing Sample**
>
> Learning About Plants and Water
>
> | First, <u>Anna placed food coloring in jars of water</u>. | Next, <u>Michael placed a white flower in each jar</u>. |
> |---|---|
> | Then, <u>we had to wait to see what would happen</u>. | Finally! <u>Each flower was the color of the water it was standing in!</u> |

 **TURN AND TALK** Writers, talk about the drawing and writing I did. Remind each other about the questions we ask to see if we have written a complete sentence. Talk about the special words in the writing that show the order of things. How did the word wall help me when I reread my work?

 **CREATE AUTHENTIC PURPOSE** Note: You may find First, Next, Then, Finally on appendix page 163 to be helpful for this.

Partners, you are going to work together to prepare your own First, Next, Then, Finally pages to share with our friends next door. You will be working together to draw and write about our experiment. Remember to ask the important questions to see if your sentences are complete after you write them. When you are finished, please use the word wall to see if you can find any of your words. Your friends in the other class will be very happy to read the writing you create.

**ASSESS THE LEARNING** As students create their illustrations and summaries, identify those students who need additional small-group support to identify complete and incomplete sentences. Pull those students into a small group to scaffold their success.

 **SUM IT UP** Writers! It is almost time to go next door and share our learning about water and flower stems. Let's think together about our writing and make sure it is the best it can be: Did you reread and touch each word? Did you use periods and sentences? Can you point to the special words that show the order of steps in our experiment? Did you use the word wall to check your spelling? Writers, I think we are ready to celebrate our learning with our partners next door.

## DAY 2 · Guided Practice

**MODEL: TRANSFER LEARNING TO ANOTHER CONTEXT** Model how to select a piece from a writing folder and how you can reread to check for complete sentences. With each sentence you read aloud, wonder: *Did this tell who did something? Did this tell what happened?* You might also model how you can check individual words against the words on the word wall.

 **TURN AND TALK** Writers, what did you see me do? Talk about the way I reread the writing and the questions I asked to check for complete sentences. Talk about the word wall and how it can help us as we reread our writing.

 **CREATE AUTHENTIC PURPOSE** Have children look at their own writing folder to select a piece to reread. Encourage them to look at each sentence and ask the two critical questions. Remind them to place a period whenever they find a sentence that answers both questions.

 **ASSESS THE LEARNING** As individuals and partners reread the pieces in their writing folders, use your class record-keeping grid to identify those who need assistance finding words on the word wall.

 **SUM IT UP** Editors, give yourselves a big round of applause! We are learning how to write complete sentences! We have learned to ask: Does this tell who did something? Does it tell what was done? We have also learned to use the word wall to check our spelling after we give it a go on our own! We have learned not to overuse exclamation points!

## DAY 3 · Support and Extend the Learning

Select experiences that will best support your learners:

- Retell familiar read-alouds by having children use the cards "First, Next, Then, Finally" to frame their retells.

- Have children create "First, Next, Then, Finally" illustrations to show sequence.

- Gather groups at the word wall and provide support in finding words from their writing.

- During a read-aloud, pause to have students think about sentences in stories. Do the sentences tell who did something and what was done? Notice the periods that show they are sentences.

# Pulling It All Together Cycle #7: Writing Questions to Ask Each Other

Question Marks • Singular/Plural • Using Known Words to Spell Other Words

### DAY 1  Model Writing for an Audience

Questions are fun to write. When we ask questions, we learn from other people. I am going to write a question across the top of my page, and then I get to be a researcher and see what I can learn. My question is: *Do you have a cat?* Notice how I use a question mark at the end so it is clear that this is a question. Let's get some answers! When I ask the question and look at you, please give me your answer. Then you can come up and write your name under the Yes or No column. (Query a few students and have them write their names on the chart as per the sample.) I am wondering if I should have said *cat* or *cats*? If I say *cats*, my question will be a little different. I won't use the word *a*. It just wouldn't sound right if I said, "Do you have a *cats*? *Cats* is plural so I would have to leave out the *a*. Which way do you think it should be? Now that I am finished writing, it is time to think about spelling. I am looking at the word *cat*. I know how to spell *hat*. *Cat* and *hat* rhyme, so I can use what I know about *hat* to check my spelling on this word.

| Modeled Writing Sample |  |
|---|---|
| Do you have a cat? |  |
| <u>Yes</u> | <u>No</u> |
| Anna | Juan |
| Alex | Tomika |

**TURN AND TALK** Writers, talk about the question I wrote. What did you see me doing? Think together about the mark I used at the end of the question and how I thought about *cat* or *cats*?

**CREATE AUTHENTIC PURPOSE** Have partners think together to come up with questions they can ask other students. Encourage them to create several questions, adding question marks, and then considering singular or plural nouns used in each question. Once there are enough questions developed so every student has one, engage the "researchers" in finding answers to their questions.

**ASSESS THE LEARNING** As partners create their questions, identify those who can utilize question marks and use appropriate forms of singular and plural. Question partners about words they know that will help them spell the words they are trying to write.

**SUM IT UP** Writers and researchers! We wrote a lot of great questions and found some wonderful answers as well. Look at all of our learning. Please remember that writers need to use question marks when they write questions, think about singular and plural to show if they are talking about one thing or many things, and use words they know to spell new words they are trying to write.

## DAY 2 Guided Practice

**MODEL: TRANSFER LEARNING TO ANOTHER CONTEXT** Use a chart created for modeled writing and show children how you can reread to search for questions.

> Are there any questions already there? Are there any you can add? Notice singular and plural. Use words you know to spell words you are trying to write.

 **TURN AND TALK** Writers, what did you see me do? Talk about the way I reread the writing. Did you see any question marks? Did you see any plurals where I talked about more than one thing? How about places where I could use words I know to help me spell other words?

 **CREATE AUTHENTIC PURPOSE** Have children look at their own writing folder to select a piece to reread with a partner. The partners need to look for singular and plural—places where they talk about one thing and places where they talk about many things. Then they should read their selections again and check for spellings they can improve by thinking about words they already know how to spell.

 **ASSESS THE LEARNING** As partners work together to reread the pieces in their writing folders, identify those who do and don't understand singular and plural. As you observe learners, notice if they are using words they know to spell new words.

 **SUM IT UP** Our list of skills we can use is getting longer and longer! We know how to use question marks, to think about words we already know to help us with other words we want to write, and to pay attention to singular and plural! Writers, give your partner a high five!

## DAY 3 Support and Extend the Learning

Select experiences that will best support your learners:

- Have children think of more questions to research. As they gain proficiency, have them change the headings on the columns to something like this: *Do you prefer apples, oranges, or grapes? What is your favorite food? Where do you ride your bike?*

- Conduct a Question Mark Scavenger Hunt. Have partners reread favorite selections and look for question marks. Mark the pages with sticky notes so they can share later.

- Create several sentences to place in a pocket chart. Structure some as questions and some as statements. Do not add end punctuation. Have the children work with you to add end punctuation to each.

- Present singular and plural forms of words on cards in a pocket chart. As you say sentences using the words, have children identify which card is the best match for the sentence. (Example: The _____ has blue petals. [flower, flowers])

- During small-group reading instruction, help children identify singular and plural forms of nouns in their small books.

- Model several pieces of writing in which your main think-aloud point is using words you know to help you spell additional words. Make it clear in your language how you are constantly using what you already know about words when you write.

- Use letter tiles to build rimes and onsets into a variety of words. If you can write *it*, you can also create *hit, fit, sit, kit,* and so on.

# Pulling It All Together Cycle #8: Creating an About the Author Page

Double Subjects • Multiple-Page Writing • Editing Checklist

### DAY 1 · Model Writing for an Audience

Note: Personalize your own About the Author page as you model for the children.

**When I publish books, they become very special to me. They have several pages and a cover, and I get my name on the About the Author page! We have been working on books with many pages, so today, I'm going to create an About the Author page to place in my book. You will see I have placed a picture on the page. Next, I need to think about things I can tell about myself. I am thinking I might say,** *Mrs. Hoyt, she loves to read and to write.* **That doesn't sound right, does it. I don't need** *Mrs. Hoyt* **AND** *she*, **because they both tell about me! It will sound better if I write** *Mrs. Hoyt loves to read and to write.* **That's better.** (Continue writing, making it clear that you will discard double subjects and not include them.) **Now that I am finished writing, it is time to use my editing checklist. I know writers reread when they are finished, so here I go. I will reread one time for every item on my editing checklist.**

Modeled Writing Sample

About the Author

Mrs. Hoyt loves to read and to write. Reading books and writing books are her very favorite things to do. Mrs. Hoyt also likes to take long walks and play with her dog.

Note: There are several checklists in the appendix, on pages 165 and 166. Select those that best match your learners.

 **TURN AND TALK Writers, talk about my About the Author page. What did you see me doing? If you were going to create an About the Author page for your book, what would you do as a writer?**

 **CREATE AUTHENTIC PURPOSE** Engage learners in creating About the Author pages. They will love it if you insert digital pictures or photocopy their class picture to place on the page. Remind them to watch for double subjects and to work with partners to use their editing checklists when they are finished.

 **ASSESS THE LEARNING** As students create their About the Author pages, identify those students whose oral and written language may still include double subjects, such as *My mom, she…* These students may benefit from small-group support with this concept.

 **SUM IT UP Writers, we have written About the Author pages. What a terrific celebration of your work as writers! Let's look at our class editing chart and think about all the things we know how to do. I am so proud of you, and I can't wait to put these About the Author pages into the books we are writing because you ARE authors!**

## DAY 2 | Guided Practice

**MODEL: TRANSFER LEARNING TO ANOTHER CONTEXT** Using a previous example of modeled writing, show children how you can reread, think about ideas, and then cut the writing into three parts to make a three-page book. Be sure to explain that each idea must be complete enough that you could make a picture. Attach each of the three sections to a separate sheet of chart paper, create an illustration for each, add page numbers and a cover, and you have—a book! Remind students that some stories might be best as two pages. Others would have four ideas and would fit on four pages. The goal is to separate the ideas so you can make one picture for each topic.

 **TURN AND TALK** Writers, what did you see me do? Did you notice how I took a one-page piece of writing and thought about cutting ideas apart so there would be three pages? Think together. How would you do this if you could?

 **CREATE AUTHENTIC PURPOSE** Have children look at their own writing folder to select a piece to reread and cut into sections that would each support an illustration. Provide them with sheets of paper, scissors, and glue. Encourage lots of rereading and discussion about pictures that would support the writing. Be sure to remind them about including page numbers as well. After they deconstruct and then rebuild their writing into multiple pages, they may enjoy creating another About the Author page. Remind children that an editing checklist may help a lot after they get their new illustrations and pages assembled the way they want them.

 **ASSESS THE LEARNING** As individuals and partners turn short pieces into multiple-page books, assess their understanding of double subject, pagination, and the use of an editing checklist.

 **SUM IT UP** Look how we are growing as writers. You can turn short stories into books!!!! Writers, give yourselves a big round of applause!

## DAY 3 | Support and Extend the Learning

Select experiences that will best support your learners:

- During small-group instruction, shared reading, and read-alouds, be sure to count pages and celebrate the number of pages used by the author!

- During shared reading, think aloud about double subjects. For example, in *The Very Hungry Caterpillar* it says, "The caterpillar ate four pickles." I am so glad the author didn't goof and write, *The caterpillar he ate four pickles!* That wouldn't have sounded very good at all.

- Celebrate the question marks in *Don't Let the Pigeon Drive the Bus* by Mo Willems, *Farmer Duck* by Martin Waddell, *Where's Spot?* by Eric Hill, and *Q Is for Duck* by Mary Elting and Michael Folsom. On chart paper, copy lines from these wonderful books and use a bold-colored pen for each of the punctuation marks.

- Use an array of editing checklists to differentiate for varying levels of development in your classroom. You will find several examples in the Assessment and Record Keeping section of this resource.

# Pulling It All Together Cycle #9: Writing a Persuasive Letter

Pronoun Order • Exclamation Points • Portable Word Wall

## DAY 1 | Model Writing for an Audience

I have been thinking it would be great to have a read-in with sleeping bags, stuffed animals, and maybe even our pajamas! We need permission from the principal, so I am going to write a persuasive letter. I have my portable word wall in my lap so I can look up letters I need. I want to make it clear this is from all of us. Should I say *me and the children*, *the children and me*, or *the children and I*? I know it is more polite to name others first, so I will say, *The children and I*. I want to use some exclamation points, too, so the principal knows we are really excited about this. Let's all sign the letter so it is clear that it is from all of us!

 **TURN AND TALK** Writers, talk about my persuasive letter. What did you see me doing? If you were going to write a letter to persuade, what could you write about? Would you like to stay up a bit late? Have you been wishing for a special story before bed tonight? How about having a friend for an overnight?

 **CREATE AUTHENTIC PURPOSE** Engage learners in writing persuasive letters to their parents. Before they begin drafting, help them select a topic. Then challenge them to use their portable word walls and exclamation points, and think about pronoun order if they are writing about someone else.

 **ASSESS THE LEARNING** As students create their letters, observe their work closely to assess their ability to use a portable word wall, insert exclamation points, and use pronoun order.

 **SUM IT UP** Writers, these persuasive letters are wonderful! You have made strong arguments for things that are important to you, plus you used your portable word walls and exclamation points.

---

**Modeled Writing Sample**

Dear Principal _____,

The children and I would like to have a special day and read all day long! We want to push back our desks and enjoy having sleeping bags and stuffed animals on the floor, too.

We think this is a very good idea since we would be doing a lot of reading! We would invite guest readers to read to us, and we would even write about the books we read.

**MODEL: TRANSFER LEARNING TO ANOTHER CONTEXT** Review previously modeled writing examples, and while children watch, identify places where you have used correct pronoun order or exclamation points. See if there is a place where you can add an exclamation point. Each time you find that you have used one of these elements, invite children to join you in celebrating!

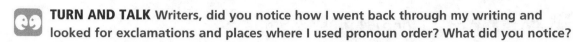 **TURN AND TALK** Writers, did you notice how I went back through my writing and looked for exclamations and places where I used pronoun order? What did you notice?

**CREATE AUTHENTIC PURPOSE** Have children look at their own writing folder to reread and look for places where they properly used an exclamation point or pronoun order. Invite them to add exclamation points if they find places where they would fit well.

**ASSESS THE LEARNING** Confer with individuals to assess understanding of exclamation points, pronoun order, and use of portable word walls.

**SUM IT UP** We are learning so much about writing! We know that when we write about ourselves and someone else, we need to be polite and list the other person first. We know how to use our portable word walls, and we are experts with exclamation points!

**DAY 3** | **Support and Extend the Learning**

Select experiences that will best support your learners:

- During read-alouds, draw children's attention to pronoun order. Some examples to consider include *A Chair for My Mother* by Vera B. Williams, *The Wednesday Surprise* and *Fly Away Home* by Eve Bunting, and *All the Places to Love* by Patricia MacLachlan.

- During read-aloud and shared reading, think aloud about exclamation points. For example, in *The Very Hungry Caterpillar*, it says, *The caterpillar ate four pickles.* Are there any places where we might take sticky notes and add exclamation points?

- Encourage children to use their portable word walls in science, social studies, math, and all curricular areas.

- During small-group instruction, encourage children to talk about things they have done with others, and support them in orally using correct pronoun order.

# Pulling It All Together Cycle #10: Writing a Description

Noticing Syllables • Singular Subject-Verb Agreement • Plural Subject-Verb Agreement

## DAY 1 Model Writing for an Audience

I am making a poster for the hallway about the bubbles we have been blowing. I am going to think about syllables to help me spell. Let's clap, *bub/bles*. There are two syllables. I know each syllable needs a vowel. I will write *b-u-b-l-s*. Hmm. I don't have a vowel for the second syllable. I will try an *e* before the *s* and see how that looks. Thinking about syllables helps me spell. I said *bubbles*. That is plural. I know because we have been talking about that. I can say, *Bubbles is floating* or *Bubbles are floating*. I am going to say, *are* because bubbles is a plural! That sounds much better! My next sentence is about one bubble. That is singular. I will need to say, *Each bubble is*....

> **Modeled Writing Sample**
>
> Bubbles are floating, shining balls of fun! Each little bubble is an air-filled wonder shimmering with color and light.

 **TURN AND TALK** Writers, talk about my bubbles description. What did you notice? What can you say about singular and plural and using syllables to help you spell?

 **CREATE AUTHENTIC PURPOSE** Have children help you create a bulletin board about bubbles. Have them blow bubbles, write as many descriptive words as they can, and then draft their descriptions. Encourage them to think about singular subject–verb agreement and plural subject–verb agreement and about clapping out words to use syllables as spelling helpers.

 **ASSESS THE LEARNING** Meet with small groups to match singular/plural nouns and verbs in a pocket chart. Identify which students can identify singular and plural nouns and select appropriate verbs to go with each.

 **SUM IT UP** I am so proud of our bulletin board. We have bubble pictures and bubble descriptions, and everyone who reads it will know how much we enjoy bubbles. I am especially proud to see that you were thinking about singular and plural and selecting verbs to match. I also noticed that many of you were clapping out your words to use syllables while you were writing. Way to go, writers!

**MODEL: TRANSFER LEARNING TO ANOTHER CONTEXT** Using a previously modeled writing, show children how you can reread your work to clap out syllables and think about spelling. As they watch, look for opportunities to add more letters after you clap and think about syllables. Reread the selection again to check for singular subject-verb agreement and plural subject-verb agreement and show children what you are noticing.

 **TURN AND TALK** Writers, what did you see me do? Did you notice how I took a moment to clap out some words and think about spelling? Tell your partner what you saw. Think together about singular and plural. What do you know? What did you notice in my writing?

 **CREATE AUTHENTIC PURPOSE** Have children look at their own writing folder to reread for syllables and singular subject-verb agreement and plural subject-verb agreement. Encourage them to work with partners and celebrate when they find things they can adjust in their writing.

 **ASSESS THE LEARNING** Gather writing samples and review for singular subject-verb agreement and plural subject-verb agreement to determine which students may benefit from further instruction.

 **SUM IT UP** Writers, we have created a wonderful bulletin board, celebrated using syllables, and spent time thinking about singular and plural! Give yourselves a big high five!

**DAY 3** | **Support and Extend the Learning**

Select experiences that will best support your learners:

- Use sticky notes to cover verbs in a guided reading selection and have children predict the verb they expect to see when the sticky note is removed. Talk to them about how noticing singular and plural helps us think about which verbs to select.

- While rereading familiar selections in small-group instruction, shared reading, and read-alouds, pause occasionally to clap out the syllables in words and think about a vowel that would fit into each syllable.

- Create a T-chart for singulars and plurals found in a familiar big book.

- Use a pocket chart to display a text that includes sentences with a mixture of singular and plural nouns. Remove the verbs. Have students talk together about verbs that would make good choices for the blanks.

- Create a Celebration of Syllables by having students orally identify words that have two, three, four, or more syllables and practice clapping them out. Have each student select one to spell, inserting a vowel into each syllable.

# Pulling It All Together Cycle #11: Writing a Book Summary

Past-Tense Verbs • Possessive Pronouns • Commas in a Series

---

## DAY 1   Model Writing for an Audience

I am going to write a book summary that I can attach to the front of *Jack and the Beanstalk*. That way, the next person who wants to read the book can read my summary and know what the story is about. As I write, I am going to be thinking about possessive pronouns (*mine, yours, his, hers, ours, theirs, whose*) because those will help me tell whom things belong to in the story. I will also think about past tense for my verbs because this story isn't happening right now. I will write *Jack traded their cow for magic beans*. *Their* tells that the cow belonged to Jack and his mother. *Traded* is a better choice than *trade* because it already happened. Jack stole a lot of things. That wasn't very nice. I am going to use commas between each item in the list of things Jack took from the giant.

> ### Modeled Writing Sample
>
> Jack and the Beanstalk
>
> Jack and his mother owned a cow. Jack traded their cow for magic beans. After his mother tossed the beans out of her kitchen window, a beanstalk grew right up into the clouds. Jack climbed the beanstalk, stole the giant's goose, his gold coins, his harp, and his food. Then, Jack chopped down the giant's beanstalk!

 **TURN AND TALK** Writers, what did you notice about my writing today? If you write a summary, which book will you choose? Which possessive pronouns can you choose? Can you think of lists you could connect with commas?

 **CREATE AUTHENTIC PURPOSE** You will be working with a partner to select a book to summarize. Read it together to remind yourselves of the most important parts. Then write a summary. It is going to be great fun to read the summaries we will have clipped to the front of our favorite books!

 **ASSESS THE LEARNING** Gather unedited writing samples and identify which students are including possessive pronouns, which students can effectively use past-tense verbs, and which students are beginning to include commas for items in a series.

 **SUM IT UP** Let's take our summaries to the library and share them with the librarian. She loves books as much as we do. I know she will be very impressed to see how you have remembered to include possessive pronouns and past-tense verbs in your summaries.

---

## DAY 2 | Guided Practice

**MODEL: TRANSFER LEARNING TO ANOTHER CONTEXT** Model how to select a piece from a writing folder and how you can reread to check for inclusion of possessive pronouns and past-tense verbs. Think aloud as you identify these elements in the writing and share your ideas about adjustments or additions you might be able to make.

 **TURN AND TALK** Writers, what did you see me do? Talk about the way I reread the writing and looked for possessive pronouns and past-tense verbs.

 **CREATE AUTHENTIC PURPOSE** Have children look at their own writing folder to select a piece to reread. Have partners work together to search for possessive pronouns and past-tense verbs. Ask students to let you know if they find any places where they could use commas in a series.

 **ASSESS THE LEARNING** As individuals and partners reread the pieces in their writing folders, use your class record-keeping grid to identify those who would benefit from reteaching in any of the understandings in this cycle.

 **SUM IT UP** Editors, give yourselves a big round of applause! You can use possessive pronouns. You can use past-tense verbs to show something already happened. You also know that you can use commas when words are in a series.

## DAY 3 | Support and Extend the Learning

Select experiences that will best support your learners:

- Read books that are written in the past tense and compare selections written in present tense. Explain to the children that writers have to decide if they are telling a story that has already happened or that is happening right this minute. (Examples: *When Sophie Gets Angry—Really, Really Angry* by Molly Bang and *When I Was Young in the Mountains* by Cynthia Rylant.)

- Model writing in which you use commas in a list.

- Have students write additional summaries of books and share them with students in other classes.

- Model writing story summaries with an emphasis on story elements so children understand that a good summary must provide information about characters, setting, problem, and solution.

- Model writing a summary of an informational text so children can see how you provide a factual summary.

# Pulling It All Together Cycle #12: Creating a Brief Animal Report

Apostrophe in Possessives • Apostrophe in Contractions • Quotation Marks

**DAY 1** **Model Writing for an Audience**

I have decided to write a brief report about the tongue of a frog. I am going to use three pages for my writing. On pages 1 and 2, I will use my own words. On page 3, I am going to pick a sentence from a book and put that sentence in quotation marks to show that I am borrowing the words from someone else. On page 1, I will write, *A frog's tongue.* . . . The tongue belongs to the frog, so I need to be sure to use an apostrophe here. That is important. On page 2, I will write, *It can't get away!* I need an apostrophe here, too, but this time it is because *can't* is a short way to say *cannot.* That is a contraction. Now, I am ready for my quotation. I chose a line from a book called *Animal Lives.* Here come my quotation marks!

**Modeled Writing Sample**

| | | |
|---|---|---|
| A frog's tongue is very long and sticky. When a frog is hungry, it waits for an insect to come by and then snaps out that long tongue and zap! | Sticky Insect Trap<br><br>The insect is stuck tight. It can't get away! | "His long sticky tongue darts out in a flash."<br><br>From *Animal Lives, The Frog* by Bert Kitchen. |
| 1 | 2 | 3 |

 **TURN AND TALK** Writers, talk about my three-page report. What did you notice as I was writing?

 **CREATE AUTHENTIC PURPOSE** Have children work with a partner or individually to create brief animal reports. Encourage them to use some of their own sentences and to consider borrowing a sentence to place in quotation marks. Explain that they will be sharing their reports with another class and, eventually, with their parents.

 **ASSESS THE LEARNING** Confer with writers to determine which students understand the use of the apostrophe for possession and for contractions.

 **SUM IT UP** These animal reports are great. You have so much to share. Take a moment and look at your work. Are all the sentences your own words? Did anyone borrow a sentence and place it in quotation marks? Did anyone use a contraction? I am really looking forward to sharing these reports with the students next door.

## DAY 2 — Guided Practice

**MODEL: APPLY THE LEARNING TO DAILY WRITING** While children watch, review previously modeled writing. Explain that you are searching for places where you might use a contraction instead of a two-word phrase. If you find a place where a contraction will work, make the change and celebrate with your writers.

 **TURN AND TALK** Writers, what did you see me do? Talk about the steps I used to help me think about this writing. What did I do to show I knew how to use contractions in my writing?

 **CREATE AUTHENTIC PURPOSE** Have children select a piece from their own writing folder. Their job is to reread and check their work to see if there are any places where they have already used a contraction or could add one. For those who are ready, ask them to reread their work to see if there is a place for an apostrophe to show possession.

 **ASSESS THE LEARNING** As individuals and partners apply the steps to the pieces in their writing folders, use your class record-keeping grid to identify those who are in control of using an apostrophe in a contraction.

 **SUM IT UP** Look how we are growing as writers. We created brief animal reports. Some of us used contractions. Some of us used apostrophes to show possession too. Did anyone select a quotation from a book to include? Good writers and editors do all of those things.

## DAY 3 — Support and Extend the Learning

Select experiences that will best support your learners:

- Provide ongoing experiences with brief animal reports so that children get used to creating short reports to show what they know. Encourage them to add boldface words, headings, titles, labels, and diagrams so their informational writing looks like the books they read for information.

- Keep track of contractions. During read-alouds and shared reading, watch for contractions. When you find one, stop, celebrate, and record it on a chart.

- Encourage children to label their belongings in their backpack, their desk, and other areas of the room with labels, such as, *Amanda's eraser, Hector's crayons,* and *Tomika's coat hook.*

- Have children create illustrations that show possession, and label them. (Examples: *This is my mom's car. This is my brother's bike. This is my father's hammer.*)

- Make a show of placing sticky notes into books with wonderful quotations and explain that you might want to use some of the phrases or a sentence in your own writing. Show the children how you borrow just a bit, placing the phrase or sentence in quotation marks.

- In big books, highlight dialogue and the speech marks that surround it. Explain how important it is that we notice the quotation marks so we know someone is speaking.

# PART IV

# Tools

The tools presented in this section are designed to be time-savers to support you and your students in creating a selection of resources that empower your work as writers.

The High-Frequency Writing Words on page 157 is an especially important resource from which you can draw words for spelling instruction, words for your word walls, and so on. These are the words most commonly used in writing, the words students need most! Use this list to power up your thinking and help you teach with maximum efficiency.

## Contents

To print out the reproducibles on the following pages at full size, please visit: www.scholastic.com/masteringthemechanics.

# Teacher Resource: High-Frequency Writing Words

This list of words represents those most commonly used in writing. Please note that word #1, *the*, occurs with the highest level of frequency while word #210, *took*, is the least commonly occurring in this high use group of words. Use this list to power up your word walls!

| | | | | | | |
|---|---|---|---|---|---|---|
| 1 the | 31 but | 61 into | 91 long | 121 another | 151 every | 181 few |
| 2 of | 32 what | 62 has | 92 little | 122 came | 152 found | 182 those |
| 3 and | 33 all | 63 more | 93 very | 123 come | 153 still | 183 always |
| 4 a | 34 were | 64 her | 94 after | 124 work | 154 between | 184 show |
| 5 to | 35 when | 65 two | 95 words | 125 three | 155 name | 185 large |
| 6 in | 36 we | 66 like | 96 called | 126 must | 156 should | 186 often |
| 7 is | 37 there | 67 him | 97 just | 127 because | 157 home | 187 together |
| 8 you | 38 can | 68 see | 98 where | 128 does | 158 big | 188 asked |
| 9 that | 39 an | 69 time | 99 most | 129 part | 159 give | 189 house |
| 10 it | 40 your | 70 could | 100 know | 130 even | 160 air | 190 don't |
| 11 he | 41 which | 71 no | 101 get | 131 place | 161 line | 191 world |
| 12 for | 42 their | 72 make | 102 through | 132 well | 162 set | 192 going |
| 13 was | 43 said | 73 than | 103 back | 133 such | 163 own | 193 want |
| 14 on | 44 if | 74 first | 104 much | 134 here | 164 under | 194 school |
| 15 are | 45 do | 75 been | 105 go | 135 take | 165 read | 195 important |
| 16 as | 46 will | 76 its | 106 good | 136 why | 166 last | 196 until |
| 17 with | 47 each | 77 who | 107 new | 137 help | 167 never | 197 form |
| 18 his | 48 about | 78 now | 108 write | 138 put | 168 us | 198 food |
| 19 they | 49 how | 79 people | 109 our | 139 different | 169 left | 199 keep |
| 20 at | 50 up | 80 my | 110 me | 140 away | 170 end | 200 children |
| 21 be | 51 out | 81 made | 111 man | 141 again | 171 along | 201 feet |
| 22 this | 52 them | 82 over | 112 too | 142 off | 172 while | 202 land |
| 23 from | 53 then | 83 did | 113 any | 143 went | 173 might | 203 side |
| 24 I | 54 she | 84 down | 114 day | 144 old | 174 next | 204 without |
| 25 have | 55 many | 85 only | 115 same | 145 number | 175 sound | 205 boy |
| 26 or | 56 some | 86 way | 116 right | 146 great | 176 below | 206 once |
| 27 by | 57 so | 87 find | 117 look | 147 tell | 177 saw | 207 animal |
| 28 one | 58 these | 88 use | 118 think | 148 men | 178 something | 208 life |
| 29 had | 59 would | 89 may | 119 also | 149 say | 179 thought | 209 enough |
| 30 not | 60 other | 90 water | 120 around | 150 small | 180 both | 210 took |

From Rebecca Sitton's *Sourcebook for Teaching Spelling and Word Skills*, 2006, Egger Publishing, Inc. www.sittonspelling.com

# Spelling Reference: Picture Alphabet Card

| Aa | Bb | Cc | Dd | Ee |
|----|----|----|----|----|
| Ff | Gg | Hh | Ii | Jj |
| Kk | Ll | Mm | Nn | Oo |
| Pp | Qq | Rr | Ss | Tt |

| Uu | Vv | Ww | Xx | Yy | Zz |
|----|----|----|----|----|----|

# Spelling Reference: Spanish Picture Alphabet Card

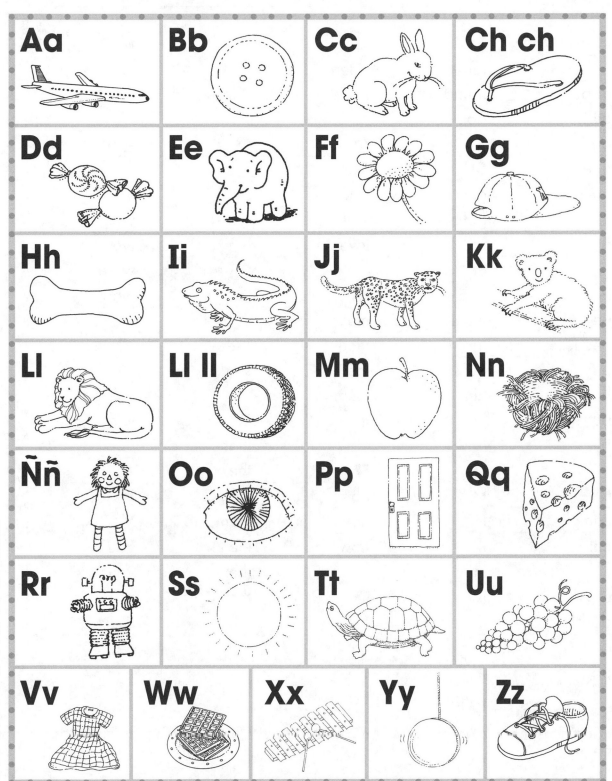

| | | | |
|---|---|---|---|
| **Aa** | **Bb** | **Cc** | **Ch ch** |
| **Dd** | **Ee** | **Ff** | **Gg** |
| **Hh** | **Ii** | **Jj** | **Kk** |
| **Ll** | **Ll ll** | **Mm** | **Nn** |
| **Ññ** | **Oo** | **Pp** | **Qq** |
| **Rr** | **Ss** | **Tt** | **Uu** |
| **Vv** | **Ww** | **Xx** | **Yy** / **Zz** |

# Spelling Reference: Portable Word Wall

This word list belongs to _____

| A | F | K | P | U |
|---|---|---|---|---|
| a | for | kitten | play | up |
| about | friend | know | puppy | |
| all | from | | | **V** |
| an | | **L** | **Q** | very |
| and | **G** | like | | |
| are | get | little | **R** | **W** |
| as | girl | look | run | was |
| at | | love | | we |
| | **H** | | **S** | were |
| **B** | had | **M** | said | what |
| be | have | make | school | when |
| because | he | many | see | where |
| big | her | me | she | which |
| boy | him | mom | | will |
| but | his | my | **T** | with |
| by | how | | that | |
| | | **N** | the | **X** |
| **C** | **I** | no | their | |
| can | I | not | them | **Y** |
| cat | if | now | then | you |
| | in | | there | your |
| **D** | is | **O** | they | |
| dad | it | of | this | **Z** |
| do | | on | to | |
| dog | **J** | one | | |
| | jump | or | | |
| **E** | | out | | |
| each | | | | |

# High-Frequency Writing Patterns/Rimes

The study of high-frequency spelling patterns, or rimes, is a sensible research-based strategy to generate hundreds of words. Several respected educators (including Wylie, Durell, Edward Fry, and Marilyn Adams) have identified the following 35 to 40 rimes that can form up to 650 different one-syllable primary words. These key rimes need to be taught and recycled continuously until the learner has internalized the patterns. Do not give the learners a list of words to memorize. Provide the learners with one word that exemplifies a high-frequency spelling pattern, like _bat_. Then remove the _b_ and replace it with _m_ to spell _mat,_ _s_ to spell _sat,_ _ch_ to spell _chat_. You are now teaching learners to spell by analogous thinking, helping them grow both as spellers and as independent learners who can augment their own words beyond a typical list of prescribed words.

| | | | | | |
|---|---|---|---|---|---|
| __ay | __ill | __ip | __at | __am | __ag |
| __ack | __ank | __ick | __ell | __ot | __ap |
| __y | __unk | __ail | __ain | __eed | __ice |
| __out | __ugh | __op | __in | __an | __est |
| __ink | __ow | __ew | __ore | __ed | __ab |
| __ob | __ock | __ake | __ine | __ight | __im |
| __uck | __um | __ump | | | |

From Rebecca Sitton's *Sourcebook for Teaching Spelling and Word Skills*, 2006, Egger Publishing, Inc. www.sittonspelling.com

From the Desk of

_____

From the Desk of

_____

From the Desk of

_____

From the Desk of

_____

# First, Next, Then, Finally

First, _____

Next, _____

Then, _____

Finally! _____

# PART V

# Assessment and Record Keeping

The assessment tools and record-keeping sheets in this section are designed as suggestions. You may find that some perfectly match the needs of your students or your personal preferences in record-keeping. We encourage you to make these tools your own or use them as springboards for the creation of tools that are just right for you and your learners.

We have deliberately tried to highlight several kinds of tools for your consideration. You will notice that there are student self-reflections in the form of I Can pages. There are sample editing checklists, a class record-keeping grid, and a blank yearlong planner.

Most of all, select the tools that will empower you to watch your students closely. Observations and ongoing daily assessments give power to instruction, enabling you to respond to the needs of individuals, gather small groups with similar needs, or select from available resources. You are the driving force in instruction. You are the only one who truly sees your students as individuals and can select supports that will lift their learning.

**Contents**

To print out the reproducibles on the following pages at full size, please visit: www.scholastic.com/masteringthemechanics.

# Editing Checklist I

Writer _____ Date _____

I Can…

| | |
|---|---|
| write my name on my paper. | ☺ |
| use sounds I know to help me spell. | ☺ |
| reread and touch each word. | ☺ |
| make sure my picture and my words go together. | ☺ |

# Editing Checklist II

Writer _____ Date _____

I Can…

| | |
|---|---|
| leave spaces between words. | ☺ |
| place a period at the end of a sentence. | ☺ |
| add exclamation points. | ☺ |
| use capital letters at the beginning of a sentence. | ☺ |
| reread to check my spelling. | ☺ |

## Strategies Good Editors Use

☐ Reread to be sure I made sense

☐ Reread to check for spaces between words

☐ Reread to add letters

☐ Reread to add words

☐ I check my work carefully.

_____  _____

(author)                                              (date)

## Strategies Good Editors Use

☐ Reread for every editing point

☐ Check capital letters

☐ Notice punctuation:

        ☐ Periods

        ☐ Exclamation points

        ☐ Question marks

        ☐ Commas

        ☐ Apostrophe

☐ Use resources to check my spelling

_____  _____  _____

(author)                       (editing partner)              (date)

# Spelling Strategies

Writer _____ Date _____

**When I come to a word I am not sure of, I usually**

_____.

**Sometimes I also** _____.

**When I am writing, I**

| | | |
|---|---|---|
| Think about my message | ☐ Yes! | ☐ Not yet |
| Listen for sounds in the words | ☐ Yes! | ☐ Not yet |
| Think about parts of the word | ☐ Yes! | ☐ Not yet |
| Draw a line under words I am not sure of and keep writing | ☐ Yes! | ☐ Not yet |

**When I am preparing my writing for someone to read, I**

| | | |
|---|---|---|
| Reread to check my spelling | ☐ Yes! | ☐ Not yet |
| Use the word wall | ☐ Yes! | ☐ Not yet |
| Use another piece of paper to try different spellings for the word | ☐ Yes! | ☐ Not yet |
| Add words to my portable word wall | ☐ Yes! | ☐ Not yet |
| Ask a friend to edit with me | ☐ Yes! | ☐ Not yet |

# Interactive Assessment

**Focus on capitalization, spelling, punctuation, grammar, spacing, or editing**

Date _____ Title of Writing _____ Author_____

**Dear Parent,**

**Thank you for joining our celebration of your student's writing. Please add your response and return this form and the writing to school tomorrow.**

**The Author**

As I look at this writing and editing, I am especially proud of _____

_____

_____

_____

_____

Author _____

**The Teacher**

As I look at this writing and editing, I am especially proud of _____

_____

_____

_____

_____

Teacher _____

**Through the Eyes of a Parent**

As I look at this writing and editing, I am especially proud of _____

_____

_____

_____

_____

Parent _____

# Skills I Can Use

| Skills used in my writing | I started using this on date_____ |
| --- | --- |
|  |  |
|  |  |
|  |  |
|  |  |
|  |  |
|  |  |
|  |  |
|  |  |
|  |  |
|  |  |
|  |  |
|  |  |
|  |  |

# Class Record-Keeping Grid

| | | | | | | | | |
|---|---|---|---|---|---|---|---|---|
| | | | | | | | | |
| | | | | | | | | |
| | | | | | | | | |
| | | | | | | | | |
| | | | | | | | | |
| | | | | | | | | |
| | | | | | | | | |
| | | | | | | | | |
| | | | | | | | | |
| | | | | | | | | |
| | | | | | | | | |
| | | | | | | | | |
| | | | | | | | | |
| | | | | | | | | |
| | | | | | | | | |
| | | | | | | | | |

# Yearlong Planner

Consider: Are there any lessons that should appear multiple times?

| | September | October | November | December | January | February | March | April | May | June |
|---|---|---|---|---|---|---|---|---|---|---|
| **WEEK 1** | | | | | | | | | | |
| **WEEK 2** | | | | | | | | | | |
| **WEEK 3** | | | | | | | | | | |
| **WEEK 4** | | | | | | | | | | |

# APPENDIX: STUDENT WRITING SAMPLES

To print out these reproducibles at full size, please visit www.scholastic.com/masteringthemechanics.

## I Am 5

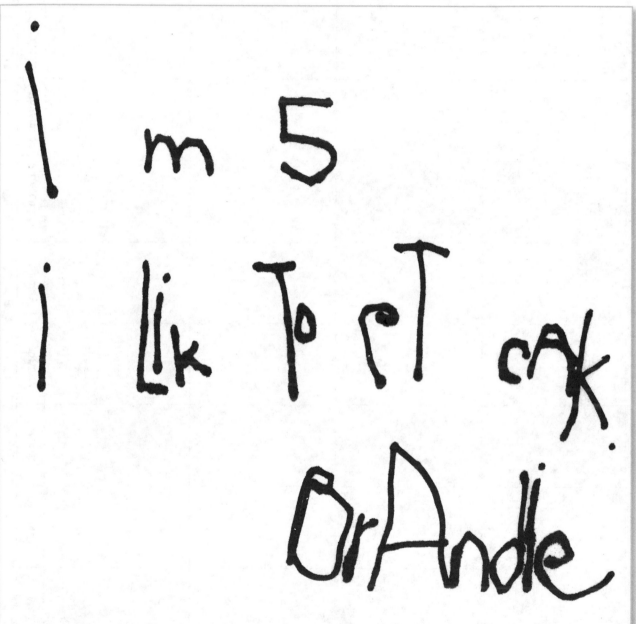

I am 5
I like to eat cake
Brandie

**The Moon Shines**

The moon sion on the Earth

If I cud fie I wd
fie hie in skie. I wd fie
ovr ~~my the~~ has. I wd wave at
~~air~~ arpane. It wd bee fun.

If I could fly, I would
fly high in (the) sky. I
would fly over my house.
I would wave at (an)
airplane. It would be fun.

## I Am Cameron

I am Cameron. I am
+ KN A WOK

CAMERON

I am Cameron.
I am taking a walk.

# My Brother

My brother is nice to me. We are frends. We like to play baskit ball. He is nice to me.

**Danny**

My dog sleeps with me in my bed every night.

I love my dog

Once upon a time there was a little old woman who loved ____ books. She arranged ____ books in every room in ____ house and filled up so many spaces that her family didn't have anywhere to place ____ own special treasures.

**Marie and I**

Marie and I both like cookies with little pieces of candy in them. One day, my mom helped Marie and me make a big batch.

**My Dog**

Brownie he likes to play catch. Brownie he jumps and runs and brings balls and sticks right back to me. I love him.

# Making a Peanut Butter and Jelly Sandwich

You need to get the peanut butter, jelly, two pieces of bread, and knife out. Spread the peanut butter on one piece of bread. Spread the jelly on top of the peanut butter. Put the other piece of bread on top of all of that. Cut the sandwich into pieces. Eat!

**Saturday at the Park**

# Saturday at the Park

It snowed on Saturday. We goed to the park. It was beautiful! I wanted to stay forever. It lookt like winter. We goded home before it got dark.

**I Love My Mom #2**

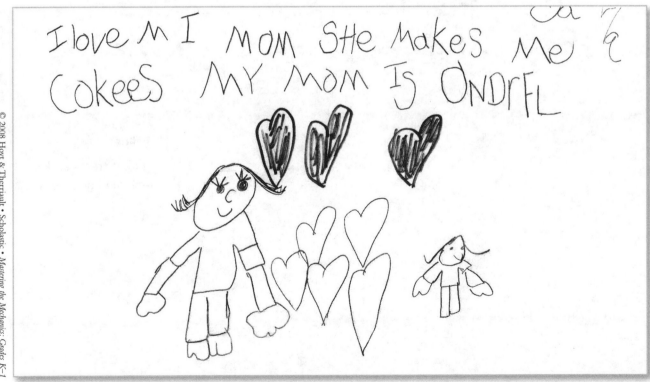

I love M I mom she makes me cokees my mom is ONDrFL

## My Poodle

Cynthia

My pet is a cine of Dog
That is a Pudole it's colre
is white and Brown. it sounds
like ruf ruf fruf. I fee Love
Abowt my Pudele. I Love
my Pudole. she Like's
chrets and evry Day. I give her a



Last line:

She likes treats and every day I give her a. . .

## Grown-Ups We Know

Team: __KATIE__
       Pete
       Jose
       Cecelia

Grown-ups we know at Elmonica School:
Some titles:    Mr.    Mrs.    Miss
                  Principal   Officer    Coach

Mrs. B
mewsik tether

Principal Homes
pricipal

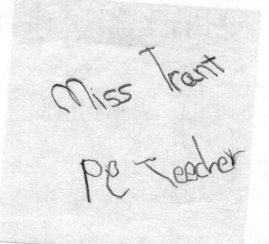

Mr. Games
my reading Budy

Miss Trant
PE Teacher

## My Grandma's House

My granmas' hous is far awae. I miss her alot! My granmas' comming to visit me. My granmas' smile is like the sun!

**Picnic**

Have you ever ben on a piknik. did ants kral in yur fud? Did it rane. I hope not?

Ryan

**Ryan's story reformatted to use three pages**

Have you ever ben on a piknik.

①

did ants kral in yur fud?

②

Did it rane. I hope not?

Ryan

③

**Alley**

Alley

In the morning my
Dad cols. Alley!
Brandy! we wack
up.

## From the Desk of

© 2008 Hoyt & Therriault • Scholastic • *Mastering the Mechanics: Grades K–1*

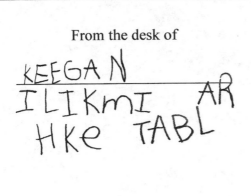

From the desk of

KEEGAN

ILIKmI AR

HKe TABL

From the desk of

ANDY

Git Sm

+OfPASt

## Pay the Nice Lady

© 2008 Hoyt & Therriault • Scholastic • *Mastering the Mechanics: Grades K–1*

MoM Pax the
nice lady the
muny and dot
For get,

## I Am Sorry

I OM

I hnsre
Fr sme

GOD BIY

I am
I am sorry
for screaming
Good bye.

**Pear**

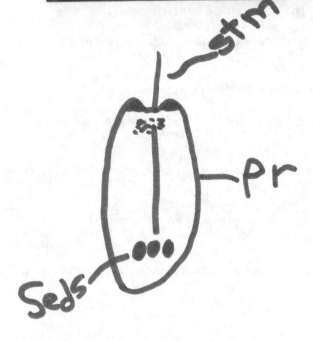

stm

pr

Seds

we ct th pr
in haf

We cut the pear
in half.

# BIBLIOGRAPHY

Anderson, J. (2005). *Mechanically inclined: Building grammar, usage, and style into writer's workshop.* Portland, ME: Stenhouse.

Angelillo, J. (2002). *A fresh approach to teaching punctuation: Helping young writers use conventions with precision and purpose.* New York: Scholastic.

Britton, J. (1970). *Language and learning.* Harmondsworth, Middlesex, UK: Penguin.

Clay, M. (2005). *An observation survey of early literacy achievement.* Auckland: Heinemann.

Calkins, L., & Louis, N. (2003). *Writing for readers: Teaching skills and strategies.* Portsmouth, NH: Heinemann.

Fletcher, R., & Portalupi, J. (2001). *Writing workshop: The essential guide.* Portsmouth, NH: Heinemann.

Gentry, R. (2007). *Breakthrough in beginning reading and writing: A powerful approach to pinpointing students' needs and delivering targeted reading and writing instruction.* New York: Scholastic.

Graves, D. (1994). *A fresh look at writing.* Portsmouth, NH: Heinemann.

Harwayne, S. (2001). *Writing through childhood: Rethinking process and product.* Portsmouth, NH: Heinemann.

Ray, K. W. (1999). *Wonderous words.* Portsmouth, NH: Heinemann.

Ray, K. W. & Cleaveland, L. (2004). *About the authors: Writing workshop with our youngest writers.* Portsmouth, NH: Heinemann.

Routman, R. (2004). *Writing essentials: Raising expectations and results while simplifying teaching.* Portsmouth, NH: Heinemann.

Sitton, R. (2006). *Rebecca Sitton's sourcebook for teaching spelling and word skills.* Scottsdale, AZ: Egger Publishing, Inc.

Topping, D. H. & Hoffman, S. J. (2006). *Getting grammar: 150 new ways to teach an old subject.* Portsmouth, NH: Heinemann.

# INDEX